P9-CCR-927

FREE OF THE SHADOWS

FREE OF THE SHADOWS

Recovering From Sexual Violence

Caren Adams, M.A.
Jennifer Fay, M.A.

Copyright © 1989 Caren Adams & Jennifer Fay

New Harbinger Publications
5674 Shattuck Avenue
Oakland, CA 94608

Edited by Nina Sonenberg

Printed in the United States
All rights reserved

First printing October 1989, 5,000 copies

Dedication

To the many women and men who have
spoken up about the daily acts of courage
recovery from sexual violence requires.

– C. A
– J. F.

Acknowledgements

Thanks to Joan Renner of the YWCA, Clark County Sexual Assault Program and to Gayle Stringer for their comments and to all those who continue the struggle to end rape and bring information about recovery to those who need it.

Thanks to Herb and Robbie, as always and to Toby, Piper, Ginevra and Elizabeth in the hopes that your daughters live in a world more free of this trauma.

Contents

What can I expect? I can't sit still. I'm frightened by everything.
How do I live with this fear and terror? He threatened to kill
me. No one knows how it feels. I can't sleep. I feel so dirty. I
don't remember what people are saying to me. How can I go
on? I'm having such a hard time deciding. How do I forget?
Why me? If only... I shouldn't have been there. Am I going
crazy?

I don't want anyone to know. Who do I tell? How can I get my
husband/boyfriend to understand it wasn't my fault? Or his?
What do I tell my children? What do I say to them? I can't tell
my family. Which friends can I trust? How will they react? I
don't want to hurt them. People say awful things. People I
didn't even tell know about it. People keep asking about the
police. People keep telling me what I could have done. Only
two weeks have passed and people expect me to be over it. I
have wonderful friends but I'm afraid I'll wear them out. What
do I tell people I'm meeting for the first time? I've got to talk to
someone, but who?

I didn't report and now I feel guilty. I made a police report and
now nothing is happening. Just when I do forget, they call and
say they have a suspect. Everything had ground to a halt and
suddenly the subpoena appears. The prosecutor doesn't return
my calls. What is going on? Does everyone believe him just
because he's willing to lie? Will I have to testify? Just thinking
about this hurts all over again. Should I testify? How can I cope
with testifying? I'm not sure I can stand it if nothing happens
to him. Is there any justice? What should I do when it is over?

It's been six months and I just seem to be getting worse. It isn't fair. Does this ever go away? What can I do besides wait? What helps? Life doesn't feel worth the effort. I can't think any more. I want to kill someone. I think I need to move or find a new job. Will I ever feel better about myself? It will never get better. No one will ever care for me now. I don't feel like doing anything. Sometimes I feel so sad. Should I see a counselor?

It happened years ago and I can't believe after all this time I want to cry. It happened to me when I was sixteen and I didn't tell anyone. I didn't know what to call it. Will they understand if I tell them now? Is there anything I can do after all this time? How do I get started? I didn't report it. I feel terrible every time I hear about a rape. Is there more I can do?

I can't even go outside for a walk. It's been a year, I was doing fine, now suddenly I'm reliving it. What's happening? I don't want to see people. How do I get over being afraid? I can't go to sleep without a long routine. It takes an hour. First I had nightmares of being attacked. Now I'm stabbing other people in my dreams. I'm so angry. I keep eating. I'm drinking too much. My credit cards are all at the limit and I'm still shopping. I just sit watching television. I'm afraid I'll become an abuser myself. I need to know how to pick a therapist and how to avoid being abused by one.

No one talks about sex. I keep hearing rape is a violent crime and not a sexual one. Sometimes when I try to make love, I feel like I'm right back in the rape again. I don't want to hurt my partner anymore, but I can't help it. This has opened old wounds. I want to make love but my partner doesn't want anything to do with me. Guilt gets in the way. I seem to be taking too many risks. What's going on? What about AIDS? I hate my body. It feels soiled, damaged.

I believed if I was a good person, people would be good to me. I don't want to look at everyone with suspicion. Is God punishing me? Am I ruined? My religion requires forgiveness. Letting go is surprisingly hard. How can I forgive those who let me down? How can I forgive myself? How do I make sense of this?

Are all men rapists? How can they do it? His friends and family defend him. How can they? Why would anyone want to do that to someone else? Are they crazy? What goes on in their heads? Will he rape again? What happens to him if he is caught? Will he come back? Does everyone who is abused become an abuser? Can I trust anyone? I still don't understand.

I'm worried about self-protection now. If I had known how badly hurt I would be, I might have made different choices. How do I decide whom to trust? I thought I could trust my feelings. I don't know how to decide. Can I ever be completely safe? I don't want to give in to the fear. I don't want to live my life in a cage. Are there no easy answers?

I can't believe it, but for days I haven't thought about being raped. I joked with my kids. I won't ever forget what happened. The world looks different to me. I'm more careful about trusting. I don't even take "victim blaming" personally anymore. I am really recovering. Maybe I can even help others.

Step by step information about how to help a sexual assault victim who comes to you, or to help a client who is assaulted while in treatment.

Please let it be a bad dream. Should I have a medical exam? What about pregnancy? Antibiotics? Can I just get the examination and not report? What if it has been days or weeks? Should I report it to the police or not?

Suggested Readings. Support Groups.

Introduction

We wish this book did not need to exist. We wish rape had ended—that no one needed to live with the fear of sexual violence. But we know the reality. In our world today the worst traumas are inflicted by one human onto another in what seems the most random way. We don't pretend to really understand how or why.

Few events are as traumatic as rape. But no Red Cross rushes in to help victims and their families live with the trauma. Crisis lines with limited time and money don't have the resources to provide as much assistance as they would like. Other people avoid victims of sexual violence out of lack of knowledge about how to help, or because of the sense of vulnerablity created by knowing a victim.

This book can help. It can't make it right or give you justice, take away the pain, or solve the dilemma of going on with a life different from the one you thought you were going to lead. But it does provide practical suggestions for getting through the days and months ahead. Suggestions for families and friends are included because recovery can be greatly helped—or hindered—by the responses of others. Fathers, husbands, boyfriends, mothers, lovers, sisters, friends and children are all faced with a crisis, a trauma, and the need for recovery, when someone they love is victimized. Often when we worked with young women in crisis, they would say, "Would you tell my father that it isn't my fault?" or "Would you talk to my boyfriend? I think he hurts worse than I do." or "I wish my mother would remember I was the one who was raped, not her."

We hope no one is recovering alone, but with the help of others. Maybe that is why you have picked this book up.

We would like to help both recent and past victims of any type of rape or attempted rape—date, acquaintance, stranger—recover from the damage those assaults usually cause. No matter what the place of the assault—your own home, at your workplace, at school, at your doctor or counselor's office—recovery requires great courage. We know from our work on a rape crisis line the tremendous pain and trauma victims often experience. Some of that pain, depression and anger are unavoidable. No amount of information can change them. But some of the destruction can be lessened if victims, their families and friends recognize some symptoms as normal, and know better how to take care of themselves and those they love. We know joy, love, happiness and a full life are still possible.

We have tried to avoid understating, or overstating the pain. We don't want to either minimize the damage rape does, or give it more power over men's and women's lives than it has already taken. Each individual suffers differently depending on the circumstances of his or her life.

We know men are directly victimized by sexual violence and rape in addition to being hurt by the victimization of those they love. Many of these pages discuss concerns common to all victims. Our hope is that whether you are young or old, male or female, you will find some help you can adapt to suit your situation. We have used the pronoun "she" simply for ease in reading.

We know reading a book about this subject when you are stressed is very difficult. We've tried to write it so you can read just one page. If you read just one page a day, much of your life will have gained some familar contours again by the time you've finished. Comforts are small when you've been traumatized, but don't give up or ignore the value of those small comforts. They can help heal.

This book is not intended as a substitute for counseling or a support group. But we know many victims cannot afford counseling, do not know of a knowledgeable counselor, or fear going to one until they know more about what they need.

The information in this book is based on many years of experience on a rape crisis line, personal experience, and interviews with experts in the fields of sexual assault and with rape victims who have reclaimed their lives.

We want most of all to provide hope: hope that this too will pass. Rape is not the end of the world. Living is better than dying. And life can be enjoyable, peaceful and exciting again.

We know the sturdiness, brilliance, grace, courage, stubbornness and anger it takes to move through to recovery.

To "recover" means to find a new balance in your life, repairing and remaking the assumptions that allow you to live with some security again. It is the accumulation of your many daily acts of courage that enable you to be free of the shadows and live fully.

How to Use This Book

We have started with the emotional reactions of the first few days. Information about medical and legal decisions usually made in the first few hours is in the appendix, since you have probably passed that point before picking up this book. We have tried to make sections stand by themselves so you can read just those sections you are interested in. Each section has notes for family and friends.

The chapter for counselors is included because many will find themselves working with a client who reports being raped. Rape is so traumatic that it assaults the assumptions of anyone who learns of a rape. It creates crisis, even at a distance. Knowledge and preparation can lessen the crisis and increase the effectiveness and ability to respond most helpfully.

1

The Nightmare

What can I expect? I can't sit still. I'm frightened by everything. How do I live with this fear and terror? He threatened to kill me. No one knows how it feels. I can't sleep. I feel so dirty. I don't remember what people are saying to me. How can I go on? I'm having such a hard time deciding. How do I forget? Why me? If only. . . I shouldn't have been there. Am I going crazy?

WHAT CAN I EXPECT?

You may have many symptoms such as restlessness, feeling out of control, physical soreness, eating difficulties; all of these are normal reactions. Ups and downs, feeling it must be a nightmare which will go away when you wake up, are all normal.

Your goal the first few days is to rest, be patient with your body, mind and feelings.

Be as patient with yourself and those symptoms as you can be.

Seeking support or counseling help through a rape crisis center may be wise to lessen the impact, and help with future decision making.

FOR FAMILY AND FRIENDS

Take care of yourself too: Although your focus is on your daughter, wife, sister, son or lover, you are in shock too.

Reach out to other friends and family as much as you can while observing the victim's wishes for privacy. You need to be able to tell others for your own support, so do not agree to a promise of total silence.

She may not show signs of shock at first. Some people cry, others don't let down at all.

I CAN'T SIT STILL

Agitation, difficulty sitting still, pacing, chain smoking or trouble being in one place are common reactions to shock and fear.

It's okay to pace, smoke, drink water and tea (endless cups of coffee probably aren't a good idea).

Don't worry about driving others crazy.

If you feel safe enough to go for long walks do that, or any other form of exercise.

You could listen to music, pet an animal, remember anything that has brought you comfort in the past.

It's okay to repeat yourself, rant and rave, ask "Why me?"

Please don't feel you need to be calm, or pretend to be okay.

FOR FAMILY AND FRIENDS

Allow her agitation. Don't ask her to sit still. If you are too tortured by the agitation, find someone else to be with her briefly while you take a break.

Try playing double solitaire with her. Any mindless time passing game can be helpful. Television may or may not be too passive or violent to be helpful. Movies carefully selected might work to pass some time.

Books with color photographs or drawings are good time-passers.

If she feels safe enough, you could take her for a drive.

I'M FRIGHTENED BY EVERYTHING

No one likes to be startled and your startle response is on a hair trigger right now. Loud noises from cars may be torture. Any hint of violence, loud music, or voices are painful.

Would music provide some cover for outside noise?

Is there a quiet spot you can retreat to?

If not, remember to slow down after you've been startled, take some deep breaths and tell yourself you are safe now.

FOR FAMILY AND FRIENDS

You can't control noise from the outside world. Be prepared to reassure her that being startled is normal. You can be careful to notice when she hasn't seen someone enter a room, or has forgotten there is anyone there, and speak to her gently.

Say to her, "You're here with me. You're safe now."

You can provide the same reassurance if she has strong reactions to sights, sounds or smells which remind her of the attack.

HOW DO I LIVE WITH THIS FEAR AND TERROR?

Fear is the most common reaction of victims no matter what the circumstances of the assault.

Your fear is as normal as an automobile accident victim's fear of riding in a car again, as a child's fear of a dog after being bitten.

Fear is primary in stranger rape, but also comes from many acquaintance assaults or date rapes. Once someone has become unpredictable, he generates the same fear. He has become a stranger to you.

Some ways to feel safer might be:

Leave lights on.
Carry a flashlight.
Put bars on the windows.
Have friends over to stay.
Move your furniture around.
Move if you can. Go home to your parents for a
    visit.
Stay with friends.
Get a dog.
Leave a television or radio playing.
Have people you can call at two in the morning.
Have a security weapon close to hand. Something
    which makes you feel more powerful and in
    control, like a rock or a hammer or a knife, can
    calm you when the fears seem overwhelming.

FOR FAMILY AND FRIENDS

Realize that some of these measures are for the *feeling* of safety. Allow that. Help her do the things

that give her some sense of safety. Your presence is
probably a great reassurance.

HE THREATENED TO KILL ME

No matter what the circumstances of the rape, the fear is there that the rapist will return or hunt for you. They rarely do, but you may feel the need for bars on windows, double-locked doors, and night lights.

At first, you may not be able to go out of your house or apartment without someone else. You don't expect that person to physically fight off anyone, you simply need the reassurance of someone else.

Rapists are less likely to return if a police report is made. If you don't make a report and you know the person, fears of his return are not unrealistic. Take some measures to protect yourself.

FOR FAMILY AND FRIENDS

Don't try to argue her out of this fear, but try not to become infected with it. You can be a source of calm and reassurance.

She just had a brush with death. It takes some time for the mind and body to absorb that shock and begin to adjust to it.

NO ONE KNOWS HOW IT FEELS

A sense of being disconnected and different from everyone else creates a sense of strangeness. Shock produces this sensation of looking out through glass at the world going by. It lessens with time. The world will probably always look different to you now. Sometimes you will see it with crystal clarity, and other times only through a dense fog.

Even through this sense of disconnection, know you can find others with similar feelings. You can call a rape crisis, or mental health, or crisis hotline to talk to someone if you feel you have no one around you to listen.

FOR FAMILY AND FRIENDS

Don't take the detachment or glassy look of non-recognition personally.

Don't—even if you have been victimized yourself—say that you know how she feels.

You can say you know it's hard for anyone else to know exactly how she feels, but that she is not alone in what she is going through. Say you care.

I CAN'T SLEEP

Turning out the lights, forgetting problems and drifting off to sleep isn't as easy now. Night may become a time of torture. When dropping off to sleep means reliving the assault, darkness is an enemy. Feeling safer can help you sleep.

During the day, explore actions or ideas about how you could feel safer. Try not to worry about being foolish or irrational. Finding a way to sleep is the goal.

Lights may help or rearranging furniture to form more of a barrier, bars across the window, an alarm system, or even getting a dog.

FOR FAMILY AND FRIENDS

Even if she was assaulted someplace other than home these measures may be necessary.

Sit with her, or lie down with her until she falls asleep.

You can establish comforting nighttime rituals such as brushing her hair or playing soft music. Don't be afraid of dependency. She just needs some comfort.

Awaken her from nightmares and reassure her that she is safe.

She may want a weapon near, under her pillow, or she may be frightened by the presence of anything representing violence. Please allow her peace of mind to come first. You may want a handgun on the nightstand, but if she feels threatened by it, you are not helping her if you insist.

I FEEL SO DIRTY

A common reaction is to feel dirty and to take baths or showers, or to wash your hands over and over again.

Bathing with strong clean herbal smells can create a sense of healing.

Picture yourself with a wound that doesn't show, but which must heal with time, just as an external wound must heal. You can see it at first as jagged, and scabbed over, and then gradually healing.

FOR FAMILY AND FRIENDS

Giving flowers may not seem appropriate but they can be comforting and clean smelling.

Soaps, bubble bath, and therapeutic mineral salts can say you know she needs to heal.

Don't worry in the first few days about what looks like unhealthy repetitive behavior such as hand-washing or many showers.

Don't be surprised if she wants to get rid of the clothes she was wearing at the time of the assault.(If the hospital or police haven't taken them for evidence.)

She may want to throw away other things that remind her of the assault.

I DON'T REMEMBER WHAT PEOPLE ARE SAYING TO ME

Difficulty concentrating continues as long as six months to a year after an attack. You may remember little of what someone says to you during the first few days or weeks. You may find it difficult to follow a conversation. You may realize someone has been talking to you and that you haven't been paying attention. It also may mean that you will go over the same ground over and over again. You discuss what you should do next, and then start the conversation all over again as if the first or second never happened. You may not notice doing this until someone seems impatient with you. It is a normal reaction to shock.

You may have difficulty speaking, too, forgetting in the middle of a sentence what you wanted to say.

Accept it. You can't fight it.

Write notes when you must remember something–even as simple as "Go back into the kitchen and turn off the oven."

FOR FAMILY AND FRIENDS

If she is aware she is drifting off, tell her it is okay and a normal reaction for anybody who has experienced a shock. Repeat yourself and the conversations as often as she repeats the cycle. Know that anything you say will need to be repeated. Expect that even everyday tasks become very difficult.

HOW CAN I GO ON?

You have commitments to work or school or a family you can't just drop. They go on, often immediately. But fear that you'll burst into tears without warning, or not be able to concentrate, can get in your way.

Sometimes you can schedule yourself to cry or grieve at a particular time of day. You may be able to stop your thoughts by saying, "At nine tonight I will sit down and consider this."

If you can establish a safe place to go when you aren't able to keep your thoughts from overwhelming you, do it.

You may need to reschedule vacation, or quit school to give yourself time to recover just as you would if you were in a severe automobile accident. It isn't fair, but sometimes that's what it takes.

FOR FAMILY AND FRIENDS

Your need to protect her may be very different from her need to go on with life. If she wants to go back to school or work, let her go, and be prepared to comfort her afterwards.

Some people can bury themselves in work. Others can work or handle other commitments and need help. Either needs to be okay. Your style of coping may be very different from the one she needs. Try to allow that difference. People recover and regain themselves at the pace they can.

I'M HAVING SUCH A HARD TIME DECIDING

Decisions about medical care, reporting to the police, or who to tell all need to be made when it is difficult to decide to eat dinner. Those around may want to take over too much or not enough. They may ask you how much help you want giving you another decision to make. "Do I want to decide this one, or let someone else?"

Ask others to take risks for you. "You make this one. I'll let you know if I'm upset." "No, don't decide for me. I'll try."

Decisions can be guided by your feelings about what you need, thoughts you have about the situation, and feedback from other people. You can ask others what they think, and decide for yourself.

FOR FAMILY AND FRIENDS

Don't assume you know what is needed or wanted. ASK. And be prepared to be told "I don't know." Accept that and make decisions on your best judgement and be prepared to be wrong.

The decision to report and follow through on legal charges can generate conflict. You may feel the legal system is the only way to find justice, and stop the rapist. She may be very frightened. You need to support what she decides to do. Statements such as "It's up to you" can feel like non-support. A more neutral statement might be, "I'll help with whatever you decide."

HOW DO I FORGET?

Over time, the memory will intrude less often. Although few people ever genuinely forget a trauma this severe, if you also actively work through feelings and fears associated with the assault, the memories will lose the quality of freshness and pain.

For now the best way to free your mind from the obsessive thoughts is to make notes to yourself about events or questions. Sometimes writing things down gets them out of mind.

After some time has passed, if you're still having trouble with intrusive thoughts or memories, you may want to get some help with specific techniques for changing thought patterns.

FOR FAMILY AND FRIENDS

Don't tell her to try not to think about it. It is normal to go over and over any traumatic event to try to make sense of it. Rape is much more traumatic than an automobile accident, the death of a loved one, or divorce.

On the other hand, if she has decided she wants to "just forget it," don't tell her she has to deal with it. Denial is a defense which protects us from thoughts or feelings too painful to handle. She may need that protection for a time.

WHY ME?

Victims of trauma rethink the events leading up to the trauma over and over again. One of the biggest questions is "Why me?"

The search for answers can easily lead to blaming the victim. The only real answer anyone has found is that the rapist was looking for a victim, and his path and the victim's path crossed. Maybe the first crossing happened days, weeks or months before, as he planned the assault, or maybe it was a one time event. Bad luck doesn't seem like a good enough answer to such an awful event, but it may be the best one.

Ask yourself how you would see it if you booked on a commercial airplane flight that crashed. If you weren't on it, you would see that as good luck. Certainly those people on it did nothing to "deserve" that fate. Yes, you can trace decisions and actions which led them there. They were on the plane "on purpose." But you certainly wouldn't blame them for those decisions.

Rape, even date rape, is nearly as random an event. Sure you can lower risks some, but not to zero, any more than the airlines do.

FOR FAMILY AND FRIENDS

You too are concerned with "Why us?" Blaming the victim is a way of avoiding dealing with vulnerability, but it isn't a real answer and does her more damage.

IF ONLY . . .

Repetitive thoughts about what you could have done differently are a defense against feelings of powerlessness and vulnerablity. If you were in an automobile accident you might say to yourself, "Yes I wish it hadn't happened. I would give anything to take back those seconds, minutes before the accident, but I can't. All I can do is take care of myself, recover and go on."

You aren't stupid because you trusted someone. Our society is based on being able to trust some people. Although some self- protection responses to rape suggest that the only answer is to be mistrustful all the time, the price of never trusting can be high too.

A rapist is a loose cannon, an unpredictable human being.

Someone who lies, breaks the law, who doesn't care about someone else has an unfair advantage over others.

You can make lists of all the actions or inactions you are holding against yourself. Once they are on paper, examine them for errors. If you could see into the future, you might make different decisions and take different risks, but from the perspective the decision was made, it was the best choice.

FOR FAMILY AND FRIENDS

You may need similar work to avoid blaming yourself.

I SHOULDN'T HAVE BEEN THERE

What if you did something "dumb" such as leaving a door unlocked, or a window open? Or were drinking, barhopping, or hitchhiking and went alone with someone you didn't know very well?

This culture is very judgmental, yet many risky behaviors are admired. Mountain climbers, daredevils, race car drivers, soldiers—they're all admired.

While smoking, riding in a car without a seat belt, and drinking and driving are finally being recognized as dangerous behavior, blaming is not the usual response. Why should leaving a window open be such an unforgiveable lapse? Must women and children live in cages? Must they be responsible for stopping rampaging elephants?

Holding rape victims responsible is a holdover from the days of women as possessions whose sole role was to remain pure.

It also functions as a form of self-protection for women who believe they would never take such a risk. Therefore they don't need to worry about being raped. Any time you hear, "Well, what did she expect," you are hearing a whining, "Not me. Not me."

FOR FAMILY AND FRIENDS

You can say, "I don't blame you or believe it was your fault." Saying "Don't feel guilty" is probably not helpful because the feelings serve a purpose. You can help change her perspective on choices. Find examples of other risks which didn't turn out badly. Affirm the nature of risks as part of life.

AM I GOING CRAZY?

The difficulty concentrating, the extreme self-doubt produced by the assault, and all the other initial reactions can lead to feeling out of control and "crazy." There is also an underlying, usually unstated myth, that if a woman was "really" raped, she goes crazy. The reactions are normal. Humans react to overwhelming stress with a certain numbness. Victims of earthquakes, hostage situations, hurricanes and war have similar symptoms.

For a very few women, being raped can be the last violent stress, which puts them in need of professional emergency psychiatric help. If feelings of suicide or extreme worthlessness are haunting your every minute, seeking emergency help is best.

Just getting through the first few days is your goal. Find people to be with you, safe ways to pass the time, rearrange furniture or closets, or play solitaire. Don't expect to do much.

FOR FAMILY AND FRIENDS

In this time-conscious culture it can be hard to just let time pass. But the goal is to put some time between the violence and the present so healing can begin.

2

You Are Not Alone

I don't want anyone to know. Who do I tell? How can I get my husband/boyfriend to understand it wasn't my fault? Or his? What do I tell my children? What do I say to them? I can't tell my family. Which friends can I trust? How will they react? I don't want to hurt them. People say awful things. People I didn't even tell know about it. People keep asking about the police. People keep telling me what I could have done. Only two weeks have passed and people expect me to be over it. I have wonderful friends but I'm afraid I'll wear them out. What do I tell people I'm meeting for the first time? I've got to talk to someone, but who?

I DON'T WANT ANYONE TO KNOW

Many rape victims try to go on with their lives without telling anyone what has happened to them or seeking help. Sometimes they don't tell because they haven't named what happened to them "rape."

You may fear the reactions of others. If you are a teenager you may have broken a rule and be certain your parents will be angry with you. If you are a young adult living away from home, you may be reluctant to tell your family for fear they will pressure you to come home again. If you are elderly and living independently, you may fear your children will use this as an opportunity to change that. If you have a husband or boyfriend you may fear his reaction.

These people can't help if you don't tell them. Going through the aftermath of rape alone, telling no one, worried about how they would respond if they knew, makes the recovery process even more difficult than it needs to be. Compassion, caring and love from others can ease the pain. Telling someone helps unload the secret and makes it less likely you will find yourself telling someone suddenly.

FOR FAMILY AND FRIENDS

Be slow to react if someone you love tells you she has been victimized. Don't look for answers. Give simple comforts, a cup of tea, time to cry, or just an ear. Give your company, attention and caring.

WHO DO I TELL?

Tell those you need support from. You may fear their reactions, but they can't help if they don't know.

Often families will ignore broken rules and understand you weren't to blame for what happened. If they are angry it's because they were powerless to protect you.

You can tell your family, "I need your help, but I am not ready to make decisions about changing my life right now."

You probably want to consider carefully what you say in your workplace. Although anyone can be victimized, you can be seen as less important, or less powerful.

You may have so much trouble concentrating at work that you need to tell your supervisor.

Some will be sympathetic and help make arrangements to ease your work load, or suggest a vacation or a leave of absence. Others will expect you to resume normal functioning after a very short recovery time. Others may still believe myths about rape.

FOR FAMILY AND FRIENDS

Offer support without telling her what she should do. Further loss of control extends the damage the rapist has done. Realize work changes may be inevitable. Acknowledge the unfairness of others' reactions. Try neither to minimize nor aggravate the sense of outrage and injustice she may experience.

HOW CAN I GET MY HUSBAND/ BOYFRIEND TO UNDERSTAND IT WASN'T MY FAULT? OR HIS?

Some men are very sympathetic and compassionate toward women who have been victimized. Some will listen to an outsider, a counselor or a rape crisis worker. Some won't listen to anyone.

You are the only one who can decide how much work or energy you have to deal with his reaction. You need people on your side. Unless the relationship is nearly over, continuing with your life without telling him is nearly impossible. Trying to maintain control all the time to hide an assault creates a strain you don't need. Unless you are certain your husband is not going to understand at all, it's better to tell him.

He may feel guilty because a car he is responsible for broke down or he left you at a party to get a ride, or for whatever reason. His guilt may help him avoid confronting how powerless he is to protect you. It takes time to be able to give up on those ideas.

FOR FAMILY AND FRIENDS

Feeling guilty or wanting to blame someone is a natural reaction when something this cruel happens. It's hard to see those we love hurt. But it is not possible to protect anyone all the time, from all possible harm.

As for sexual jealousy: You have heard that rape is a violent crime, not a sexual crime. The truth of this statement is in the reality for the victim. She feared for her life.

WHAT DO I TELL MY CHILDREN?

The best way to talk with school-aged children about rape is to be direct and matter of fact:

"Someone broke into the house and raped me. I am going to be okay."

Many children have learned about sexual assaults in school safety programs or seen television programs about rape. They are likely to know that something has happened and will be better off having concrete information and being able to ask questions.

They may sense your distress and that you aren't available to them. They may even behave badly to try to get your attention. You will need support responding to their needs.

Sometime when you have had a chance to heal you may want to talk about what happened to you as part of a discussion of making choices about personal safety. In the first few months though, simply tell them you are going to need some time to recover, but that you will be all right. You might think of little things they can do for you so they have some sense of contribution to your recovery.

FOR FAMILY AND FRIENDS

Provide support, reassurances about safety and attention to the children to the extent you can. If you are too distracted to provide it, find a friend or family member to back you up. What the children know should be under her control. Children should be given permission to be happy even if she is still sad.

WHAT DO I SAY TO THEM?

You may wonder not so much *who* to tell, but *how* to tell those who are important to you what happened. Tell them you were raped. Don't feel you must tell details or specifics. You can tell them as much about the circumstances as you choose, and you can say, "I don't want to say any more than that right now."

You may be pressured to talk about it, or you may feel your family is intrusively curious. They're trying to understand what happened and probably believe knowing details about the rape will help them understand. Tell them you don't understand either, but it's too painful to go into details. Talk about your feelings, in response to pressure to talk. Or tell them you are trying not to feel anything right now, but you appreciate their efforts to help.

The exception to not talking about the details of the assault is if the need to testify comes up and you know some of the details will be upsetting.

FOR FAMILY AND FRIENDS

You can say any combination of:

I'm really sorry this happened to you.
I don't understand how someone can be so cruel
    to someone else, but I know it happens.
I know you're really hurt. I will be patient.
I care about you.
I believe you.
I'm here with you.

I CAN'T TELL MY FAMILY. WHICH FRIENDS CAN I TRUST?

You can trust friends you have already talked with about rape who know that it could happen to anyone. You can often trust others who have been through difficult times and have learned how unpredictably they can strike. You can trust others you have seen react to problems without judging or denying.

Friends can be unpredictable. You cannot assume a woman will understand better than a man, or that someone "liberal" will have enough knowledge about rape not to blame the victim. Some women are really afraid. They fear if it could happen to you, it could happen to them, so they may try to find fault with your actions, or look for things you did that they would never do.

Good friends, maybe new ones, maybe old, will stand by you through everything. They will take your children until you are ready to care for them again. They will ask you to stay with them until you're ready to move or go home. They are the ones who tell you to call at two in the morning and mean it.

And they are the ones who will call to check on you even if they don't hear from you. Finding these friends means you'll need to tell enough people to find the ones who will stand by you.

FOR FAMILY AND FRIENDS

Remarks questioning the victims' actions, or her perception of reality are hurtful. Don't say, "Are you sure that's how it happened?" "I don't understand how that could be," or even "You'll be fine."

HOW WILL THEY REACT? I DON'T WANT TO HURT THEM.

Most families are supportive once they get over the initial shock. Of course you are reluctant to hurt them, and you know the news will hurt, but they can help only if they know. Most want to know, and help. But they may be ashamed and want to find a way this hurt and pain could have been avoided. That can sound as if they blame you for what has happened. Most families live on the idea that good behavior is rewarded and bad punished. Some have a hard time acknowledging that the world doesn't operate fairly. Many families are very supportive, and know that rape is one of the realities of the world which cannot always be avoided.

They might not say very much. No one quite knows what to say to a victim of sexual assault. Respect for your privacy may make it seem best to say nothing, unless you bring it up.

You need to cling to the knowledge that you did not create the pain. The rapist created the cruel hurt and shock. You were hit by the first wave of it, and those close to you who care about you are hit by a second. But you are not the source of the hurt or the crisis.

FOR FAMILY AND FRIENDS

Take some clues from her. If you ask how she is feeling or doing or sleeping and she doesn't respond, back off a little bit. You can continue to offer day to day security and comfort without intruding.

PEOPLE SAY AWFUL THINGS

You are very vulnerable to slights and hurts right now. You may remember something someone said for much longer than it deserves. People may not realize how sensitive you are and are often clumsy about what they say.

You may have had some unpleasant experiences after making some of the initial decisions. A police officer may have said something which sounded blaming; the medical examination may have seemed cold and impersonal. Because you were in crisis, these events hurt even more than they would normally—your defenses are down during a crisis.

You may be able to detoxify blaming remarks symbolically. Try writing them down, and then tearing the piece of paper into shreds. Try writing a dialogue with the officer, doctor, nurse or whoever said the hurtful remark. Tell him/her exactly why they don't know what they're talking about.

Blaming the victim and sexual labeling sometimes happens in high schools. Sometimes it goes with an obnoxious come-on such as "Now that you're not a virgin anymore."

Handling name calling when you are so vulnerable takes enormous effort. Name calling is part of the garbage of a society too afraid to understand. When you are approached directly it's almost impossible not to be defensive, but ignoring comments *is* the best response. Unless you decide that being shocking or rude will help you feel better. That is after all the point, not to preserve their stupid feelings, but to help you feel better. Would it feel better to say, "How can you be so certain you know everything?"

FOR FAMILY AND FRIENDS

Hearing your loved one talk about further hurts is painful. And it's more tempting to react for her because the attacker is known. Ask yourself what she wants. Does she want reassurance that the labels are false? Does she need help deciding how to react? What to say? Or does she need even more help to make a move to a different school, or to a new job?

PEOPLE I DIDN'T EVEN TELL KNOW

You may have less control over who knows you've been assaulted than you would like. Reporting to the police sometimes results in a small story in a newspaper which simply says, "Rape reported." Other times, for lack of other news, or because yours is one of a number of serial assaults, stories are run which seem to lack only the victim's name in identifying details. (Few papers report victims' names.) Even an unreported rape often reaches the ears of someone unwilling to respect a victim's privacy. You then end up having to cope with two problems: who to tell yourself, and how to react to those who know and don't respect your need for privacy.

Your mother's friends come up to you and say something like, "I'm really sorry" but you haven't told them a thing. What do you say? Although you're likely to feel funny about this unasked for sympathy or pity, getting angry with these people will increase your sense of being out of control. A simple answer like, "I'm getting better" or "Yes, it's difficult" will get you by. You need not respond to any futher remarks or questions, like "I'm sure it was dreadful." The temptation may be to say, "You have no idea." A better response would be a simple "Yes." Think of yourself as a widow, or the victim of a hurricane. Even in those cases people say stupid things, and can be unbelievably snoopy. If you have one pat answer to all circumstances, it will be much easier to give it when someone surprises you with an intrusive remark.

FOR FAMILY AND FRIENDS

Don't promise to keep the assault a secret. You need to be able to talk to others. At the same time, let those folks know what response to the victim seems most helpful. A simple, "I'm sorry to hear what happened," is usually enough.

PEOPLE KEEP ASKING ABOUT THE POLICE

People want to believe there is justice in the world, and television leads people to believe that the police will go out and get the rapist and something will happen. You may not have reported to the police, or delayed reporting, or the police may not have been interested.

Practice some responses:

"Yes, I reported. We're waiting. I don't know what the police are doing."

"No, I didn't report."

You don't need to explain yourself. Most people do not understand how the criminal justice system works. You probably can't explain it because it doesn't correspond to the picture people cling to for their own security needs.

People may also ask if you are getting counseling. People want to feel you are receiving professional care, both out of concern for you and because it relieves their responsibility. No matter what your plans are about counseling, you will want a response which leaves you in control.

"I'm well informed about my choices. I'm considering what is best for me."

FOR FAMILY AND FRIENDS

You will also be questioned about the police and counseling. Practice your own answer. You are not required to explain anything either. Tell people you appreciate their concern. Leave the conversation when it turns an unappealing direction.

PEOPLE KEEP TELLING ME WHAT I COULD HAVE DONE

Practice a few lines for those who are too ignorant to understand that a rape victim may be too terrified and disbelieving to put self-protection devices to use, or that they may not work. "No one expects to be raped." "I did the best I could." "Maybe you could do that. I couldn't." "Had I known ahead of time what was going to happen I might have done that."

Although it is very difficult not to be defensive, the less you argue with people, the more in control you will feel. It is usually not possible to convince them they don't know what they're talking about. They are often protecting their own beliefs which allow them to live in comfort in a dangerous world.

FOR FAMILY AND FRIENDS

Reassure her that no one knows how they will react until they are in a situation. Each person makes the best choices she/he can. No one else can second guess them.

You may need to respond to those who ask why she didn't fight more. You can try to educate people if you have the energy. Rape victims fear for their lives and many believe surviving the attack, not avoiding the rape is their only path."How do I get through this alive? How can I keep him from hurting me or the baby or someone else? How am I going to get away once this is over?" are the questions most in their minds. The physical force may range from threats to life endangering. That doesn't change the reality for the victim: terror.

ONLY TWO WEEKS HAVE PASSED AND PEOPLE EXPECT ME TO BE OVER IT

Family, or a lover, may feel that if you simply pretend it never happened, it will go away. This may fit with what you want for a time, but may leave you cut off from the sympathy, caring and help that would help you recover better.

Somebody may tell you to keep your chin up, or keep a stiff upper lip, or something like that. "Be strong" is in the same category as "Don't let them get you down." These are meant to be helpful and may be the other person's way of responding to crisis and problems. They may indicate a lack of understanding of how severe the trauma of rape is, or a desire to minimize it.

Ignore these comments if possible. You can respond by saying that isn't your way of handling problems. You could say to yourself, "Where do I *find* a stiff upper lip?

You want a phrase your mind can latch onto instead of being hurt and controlled by others who don't understand. You want to create phrases to go around in your head instead of letting others put the words there.

FOR FAMILY AND FRIENDS

It is upsetting and overwhelming to see someone you care about in pain when you lack a way to help very substantially. Minimizing the trauma or hoping it will go away is natural. You will need to fight that impulse for yourself and the one victimized.

I HAVE WONDERFUL FRIENDS BUT I'M AFRAID I'LL WEAR THEM OUT

Don't be afraid of overloading your friends. Don't let that fear stop you from talking about an assault as often as you need to.

Some traumas are dealt with by repeated telling of an event. Veterans need to tell their war stories over and over again. Storm or flood victims repeat the fear and terror. Certain details will remain peculiarly vivid.

Call supportive people when you need help. Ask them to call you. Let them know they are helping you and they will hang in there longer with you.

You need people who encourage your growth and courage while sympathizing with how hard it is.

FOR FAMILY AND FRIENDS

You'll get tired. You'll find yourself wishing she could get better faster. You may feel guilty about feeling good or okay when she doesn't. The better you take care of yourself, the better you will be able to keep responding as long as needed.

WHAT DO I TELL PEOPLE I'M MEETING FOR THE FIRST TIME?

While recovering from a rape, or reprocessing an old assault, the sense of victim as a primary identity can be overwhelming. Meeting new people creates a dilemma. Do you tell them so they can better understand why you react in particular ways? Do you use this as an opportunity to shake that identity and go on with life? The second is an attractive alternative except that you may end up feeling like a hypocrite or stranger to the group. The assault is the most important thing in your life right now, and not talking about it may make everything seem phony and trivial.

FOR FAMILY AND FRIENDS

Allow her to make the decision about telling new people in your life about the assault. Understand the conflict for her between telling and staying quiet. If the choice turns out badly, avoid second guessing her.

I'VE GOT TO TALK TO SOMEONE, BUT WHO?

If you are reluctant to tell someone close to you you might try a:

- a rape crisis line
- a mental health hotline
- a family planning or sexuality counselor

You can tell these people the unpleasant details that are are haunting you, but you don't want to reveal to your family or a lover.

One of the most healing processes is to find a group of women who have experiences similar to yours. No two experiences are the same, but realizing you are not alone can be an enormous relief. Hearing how others respond to remarks, demands, etc. can help lessen the pain.

FOR FAMILY AND FRIENDS

Others more distant can give her room you can't provide because you are too close. Try not to feel left out if she needs to turn to others or if she turned to others before she found the courage to tell you.

3

Justice marches to a Different Beat

I didn't report and now I feel guilty. I made a police report and now nothing is happening. Just when I do forget, they call and say they have a suspect. Everything had ground to a halt and suddenly the subpoena appears. The prosecutor doesn't return my calls. What is going on? Does everyone believe him just because he's willing to lie? Will I have to testify? Just thinking about this hurts all over again. Should I testify? How can I cope with testifying? I'm not sure I can stand it if nothing happens to him. Is there any justice? What should I do when it is over?

I DIDN'T REPORT AND NOW I FEEL GUILTY

The FBI estimates that only one out of ten rapes is reported to the police. Most rapes are not reported.

You may have known the assailant and been afraid of how the police or your family would respond. You may have been doing something illegal or against the rules when victimized; underage drinking is common, as is the presence of illegal drugs. Your community may lack confidence in the police. The rapist may have threatened to kill you if you reported him. You may not have wanted to go through police reporting and a medical examination. You have the right to make that choice.

The rapist's behavior is not your responsiblity.

When women do report to the police it increases the possibility that a rapist will be caught and possibly sent to jail. But it is far from 100% certain. Multiple reports can help piece together information when a serial rapist is attacking. Reporting a crime is a civic—and some would say a moral—duty. But it is a choice each person must make.

Victim's Compensation, money to pay for medical or mental health services, is only available to those who make a police report.

FOR FAMILY AND FRIENDS

Reporting an assault to the police means remembering and talking about the victimization. The decision to do that should be left as much as possible to the victim. Respect her choice not to report if that is her decision.

I MADE A POLICE REPORT AND NOW NOTHING IS HAPPENING

If you reported to the police, you may not know what to expect next. What happens after a police report is made is different in each case.

Often interviews with detectives and district attorneys (called prosecutors in some counties) will be required. Nothing may happen for long stretches of time depending in part on whether or not the rapist is caught right away, or on the attorney's schedule.

At some point in the process, the grand jury, or district attorney or prosecutor, may decide there is not enough evidence to continue the case. You may feel very let down if the rapist is never caught, or the system does not prosecute.

You may run through thoughts of revenge, vigilante action, and despair. If you have believed in the criminal justice system's response to this crime, you suffer a major loss of security to realize people can commit such crimes and not be punished. Many people who encounter the criminal justice system after a sexual assault have felt the same sense of betrayal.

FOR FAMILY AND FRIENDS

You may have the same feelings of anger, or need for revenge. You may feel this more or less than she does. Many victims are frightened by further violence. They may want something to happen, but they don't want you to initiate it: certainly not if you're going to end up in trouble yourself. Don't cause her to worry about your safety too.

JUST WHEN I DO FORGET, THEY CALL AND SAY THEY HAVE A SUSPECT.

Dealing with the legal system means being out of control. Calls for interviews, for legal action, come at odd times, and often as a total surprise.

If the rapist was a stranger you may have to view a lineup. Lineups can be frightening and upsetting because it is the first time you will see the attacker again. Don't go alone. The person who goes with you will not be able to be right next to you during the lineup, but at least will be there for support afterward.

If your area has a Victim Assistance Unit in the prosecutor's office or a Rape Crisis Center, an advocate can help explain what's going to happen, and what the "likely" process is. They can't make the system work differently, but at least you may have a better idea of what to expect, and what your rights in the process are.

FOR FAMILY AND FRIENDS

During the entire legal process, you too will feel bounced around. You will be excluded from some proceedings, informed and included in others. You will need to be respectful of the victim's privacy even though you want to know more about what is going on.

EVERYTHING HAD GROUND TO A HALT AND SUDDENLY THE SUBPOENA APPEARS. THE PROSECUTOR DOESN'T RETURN MY CALLS. WHAT IS GOING ON?

The legal system operates at its own speed, and with its own purpose—much of which is based on protecting the rights of the accused. Recent reforms have been aimed at providing more information to crime victims, but they are rarely adequate.

Be persistent in phone calls. Ask to be notified if the defendant (or accused) is released. Ask to be included in plea bargain decisions. Some jurisdictions do this now.

Most of all know that very little of what is happening happens because of who you are. It is not personal. It is not aimed at you. It is because of the orientation of the system.

FOR FAMILY AND FRIENDS

You may be just as bewildered by the legal system. Remember that lawyers go to school for years to understand the system and even they may not know what is going to happen next. Sometimes dividing phone call tasks helps distribute the work. You may feel left out or excluded from the process at the same time as you are being asked to provide support which stretches your resources.

DOES EVERYONE BELIEVE HIM JUST BECAUSE HE'S WILLING TO LIE?

Rape victims often feel they are on trial, instead of the rapist, even with laws written to protect past sexual history. You are the principal witness and that can make it seem as though it is your job to prove it happened. Criminal lawyers employ private investigators who may question neighbors or relatives you didn't tell about the rape, in an outrageous invasion of privacy.

Often when a rapist is caught, he is free during the pre-trial and trial proceedings. Often he is released on his own recognizance (meaning he wasn't even required to post bail).

You may learn what the defense is: this defendant is the wrong person; or you consented; or the victim made up the story for revenge, to stay out of trouble, or to get attention. No one expects to be called a liar, especially in a formal setting.

You may know the offender's family, or they may have contacted you to pressure you to drop the charges against their child, husband, father. Sometimes community groups organize to defend someone. You can feel very alone. Remember that you have support too. It may be less organized, it might be quieter, but it's there.

FOR FAMILY AND FRIENDS

Reassure her that you continue to believe her, even when it appears no one else does. You will need to assess when sympathizing will be most helpful and when providing some balance to her sense of injustice will help.

WILL I HAVE TO TESTIFY?

Most rape or sexual assault victims never find themselves faced with testifying at a trial. Either the rapist isn't caught, or he plea bargains to a lesser charge, or the prosecutor declines to file criminal charges. Sometimes when the offender has committed a previous crime, the outcome is determined by a parole hearing instead of a trial. Even if you don't testify, you may spend time thinking you will need to.

For those who do testify, it can happen any time from three months after the attack to years later. The waiting is difficult. You can't begin the real forgetting process until after the case is settled. The legal action may be very out of synch with your personal healing process. One way to deal with waiting for a trial is to write down everything you will want to remember at the time, and then refuse to think about it until it happens.

Testifying in the hopes of convicting a rapist is a brave civic action. It will not necessarily bring you justice or satisfaction—but it might.

FOR FAMILY AND FRIENDS

It is difficult to assess how testifying and appearing in court would affect someone. For some it is a time to be heard and believed, a chance to say, "I am not his victim any longer." Some feel a chance to regain control of their lives through the legal system.

JUST THINKING ABOUT THIS HURTS ALL OVER AGAIN

Crying is a normal, healthy response to having to relive the assault. Rereading police statements and remembering the details of the assault can start flashbacks and nightmares again. Trials never occur at convenient times. You may have recently returned to a comfortable routine. You can return to that again after the trial. It will not be as difficult to re-establish yourself the second time (or the third, or the fourth.)

Your sense of faith in the legal system may be shattered even as you're being asked to "play the game."

You may fear seeing the assailant again. Seeing a rapist is a shock. A clean shaven, dressed up man does not match our internal picture of who a rapist is. In the formal rational setting of the courtroom it can be hard to believe that the person you see really did what you know he did. If you know the offender, or he is a relative, the difficulty can be even greater. Try to decide what comforts or rewards you can provide yourself or ask for from others. Try to arrange those even on days you appear at the courthouse and the proceedings are delayed. You need to reward yourself for your effort even if you were not able to do what you prepared to do.

Set a time outside the courthouse where you can be as outrageous, rude, angry, and eccentric as you like, just to get a chance to express yourself.

FOR FAMILY AND FRIENDS

You may be as shaken as she is. This isn't easy. She needs your support for going through with this.

You may feel resentful that just when everything seemed to be better she's been thrown back into the terror and nightmares again. She needs you more than ever as she is subjected to public scrutiny. If she chooses to do this, support her courage.

SHOULD I TESTIFY?

To testify as a rape victim takes great courage.

A courthouse is unknown territory to most people. The beginning of the trial is almost always delayed at least once. Once the trial starts it isn't usually known exactly when you will testify. In many cases you will not even be allowed in the courtroom until after your testimony, and if your family is testifying, they too may be excluded. The wait before testifying can be long: sitting in hallways, feeling conspicuous.

When it is time to testify, you will sit in the witness chair, face the defendant(s) and maybe a jury and tell about events you have been doing your best to forget. Describing the attack in the courtroom probably will take you right back into the rape. Promise yourself a reward for testifying. Win or lose, testifying is a brave act.

Testifying is making a public statement. Some of the tools used by public speakers to help overcome anxiety can help you to: think about how you want to answer some of the questions you may face from the defense attorney.

Decide what you are most afraid of: facing the rapist(s), crying, going blank, or something else. Then decide how you'll handle it when and if that happens.

Know why you have agreed to testify so you can remind yourself. "I am here because I want to stop this person from hurting anyone else." Or, "These men need to know they can't just brutalize someone and laugh about it."

FOR FAMILY AND FRIENDS

Ask her if she wants you in the courtroom. If she would rather not worry about the effect of her testimony on you, arrange for someone to be in the courtroom she is comfortable with. If you listen to her testimony, be prepared to be emotionally bombarded again.

HOW CAN I COPE WITH TESTIFYING?

Becoming numb, fatalistic or despairing is not the goal. Real emotion conveys genuineness. But you can decrease the level of anxiety and panic to a bearable level with these steps:

1. Find a support person. Be sure there is a friendly face in the courtroom besides the attorney. Your family may not be able to be in the courtroom, or you may feel badly about having your family dragged in. Sometimes the defense pounds on them, to lessen their credibility. It can be very difficult not to feel like that is your fault. But it isn't, and your family wouldn't do it for you if they didn't want to.

2. You will probably review your testimony with the prosecutor (if he or she doesn't arrange for do this, complain). The prosecutor often gives these tips: be honest, be respectful, call the judge "Your Honor," speak to the jury. You may be asked to control your anger, and not to be rude.

3. You can visit the courtroom ahead of time. Find a parking spot, or the right bus to take. Sit in the judge's chair (at lunch hour). Watch another trial.

FOR FAMILY AND FRIENDS

Reassure her that you and the other witnesses on her behalf want to be there for her. Remind her that you feel better doing something about what happened. That you too want to help gain safety from the offender.

I'M NOT SURE I CAN STAND IT IF NOTHING HAPPENS TO HIM.

All through this, it has probably seemed to you that it has been harder on you and the people you care about than it has been on the offender. If nothing happens to him, it can be hard to adjust to the lack of consequences when you have paid such a high price, and continue to pay. Why does nothing bad happen to him? Couldn't he at least go through as much as you have?

Don't expect to find that balance from the legal system. Don't count on anything having to do with the offender making you feel better. Even if things were perfect with our system and he suffered, that does not take away the sexual violence and damage to you. Don't look to the legal system to "fix" what happened. It might punish him, it might not. Either way, your recovery does not depend on it. Your well-being should not be linked to his. The legal process is just one step in your recovery.

FOR FAMILY AND FRIENDS

Don't link *your* well-being, either, to the outcome of a legal process. Help her to do her best and be proud of that.

IS THERE ANY JUSTICE?

The system, even when it works well, does not change the injustice to you.

The picture of the criminal justice system painted here is grim. Many within the system are aware of the difficulties the criminal justice system presents to crime victims, especially victims of sexual assault. Many are doing their best to lessen the trauma. But the system is set up to safeguard the civil rights of the offender, not to protect the victim. Because of the myths surrounding the crime of rape, and the level of trauma of sexual assault, the criminal justice system is probably most traumatic for those victims.

Your experience may be much more positive. Being prepared for the worst, however, can lessen the shock and surprise and allow you to cope better with whatever you encounter.

If the offender is punished and that is what you wanted, you may gain some sense of satisfaction. But you still have your own life to repair. Sometimes it comes as a real shock if you aren't aware that the pain continues even after the trial is over. And much of the personal support around you may end when the trial is over. The end of the stress and anxiety can be a real letdown.

If the offender is not found guilty, an additional injustice is added to an already nearly intolerable load. You may have the legal option of a civil suit. If you caused the offender to face questioning you created some difficulty for him, but rarely does that feel like enough.

FAMILY AND FRIENDS

Don't make the mistake of thinking it's over once the legal proceedings end. She still needs your support in putting this behind her, especially if the offender was never found, or not convicted. Help her to separate herself and what she knows to be the truth from what the system did.

WHAT SHOULD I DO WHEN IT IS OVER?

No matter what the outcome—acquital, charges dropped, or conviction—celebrate when it has reached some sort of end point. You deserve to mark this occasion as important. You have been through a lot. You acted in a daring and courageous way. You defied the person who hurt you, to the best of the ability of the legal system. For that, you deserve credit.

Even if it feels odd, celebrate because you did your best, tried your best, did all you could within the limits of the criminal justice system. You did cause trouble. You did place the blame where it belongs. If someone else accuses him, a record will stand. Even if he was acquitted, many people are aware that guilty people escape conviction due to circumstances or lack of evidence, or a disbelieving judge.

FOR FAMILY AND FRIENDS

Help her celebrate: a card, a gift, a special dinner, a bonfire of legal papers. Help her not to get stuck if the legal system failed to bring justice. It may feel like yet another loss, but move on.

4

Daily Acts of Courage

It's been six months and I just seem to be getting worse. It isn't fair. Does this ever go away? What can I do besides wait? What helps? Life doesn't feel worth the effort. I can't think any more. I want to kill someone. I think I need to move or fine a new job. Will I ever feel better about myself? It will never get better. No one will ever care for me now. I don't feel like doing anything. Sometimes I feel so sad. Should I see a counselor?

IT'S BEEN SIX MONTHS AND I JUST SEEM TO BE GETTING WORSE.

Weeks or months have passed since the assault, and you think you should be better than you are. Or, you are depressed much of the time, and badly startled by incidents of sudden fear and flashbacks.

The pain caused by sexual victimization has been underestimated by this society for a long time, but it is very real. Accepting how badly you have been wounded may be too overwhelming. Denying the damage is one way the mind protects you from being overwhelmed.

Denial means that even while your life is falling apart, you fail to link that to the victimization. You blame yourself for everything going wrong. You wonder if you have gone crazy, or become stupid. You haven't. You are suffering the normal symptoms of shock and stress.

Some of the suffering of rape victims comes from the notion that if you are not happy, if you experience personal grief or trauma, it is your fault. Often others have little time or tolerance for the natural reaction to such a traumatic event.

FOR FAMILY AND FRIENDS

Recovery from rape takes time: it takes effort; it takes willingness to feel pain, anger and a range of emotions generally considered unacceptable.

Recognize that recovery occurs in stages with many "relapses." Try to allow room for negative emotions. Know that you have your own rhythms of response which will often be out of synch with hers.

IT ISN'T FAIR

Rape creates loss: loss of innocence, loss of the belief that the world is a good place where good things happen to good people, loss of a sense of security, loss of dreams, and loss of the time it takes to recover. And loss of self-image, and loss of the life you were leading. You may feel robbed of the characteristics which helped you feel lovable: your niceness, your trust of others, your easy laugh. It's hard to imagine that you will find new ways of being, new courage, patience, and a new sense of reality to allow you to feel lovable again.

Suddenly, you are living a life not of your choosing. Any experience changes you. But this one has so many negatives, it is typical to wail, "It's not fair." It isn't fair. There is no way to say that strongly enough. And yet, your task is to find ways to harness that sense of injustice, keep the knowledge of the injustice, while you find ways to go on. Going on, finding ways to live fully in the face of fear, loss, pain, and uncertainty is courageous, in whatever measure it is done.

FOR FAMILY AND FRIENDS

You too are struck by the unfairness. Most people already have all the problems they feel capable of handling. They don't need any more. And out of nowhere comes another, a giant. If you ignore it and just go on, you leave the victimized one coping alone. You can check with her at regular times, once a day/week/month. Tell her you are thinking of her; ask if she would like to talk, or go somewhere together.

DOES THIS EVER GO AWAY?

Those counselors who work with people suffering losses suggest three stages of recovery. It may help to know what those are, although they are rarely gone through smoothly or in order.

The first stage is shock/denial. This initial crisis stage is a time when you feel numb, unable to believe the reality of what has happened to you. Your mind is protecting you as well as it can from the terrible hurt you have suffered. You may appear to others to be fine. As the numbness wears off, other kinds of denial begin. A denial that the rape really hurt you; a denial that the person who raped you can continue to cause so much pain; a denial that the pain, the despair, the fear is real.

The next stage is anger/depression. This seems to be a stage of fighting with, or attempting to bargain away what has happened. It is a struggle of unexpected emotional reactions and a continual sense of grayness.

The third stage of recovery is understanding/acceptance. This sounds contradictory when talking about rape. How can you understand or accept rape? That's what is so tricky. You can't accept what has happened to you as "okay" or "deserved" or understand the rapist so much that he is relieved of responsiblity. It is, instead, accepting the reality of what has happened to you.

FOR FAMILY AND FRIENDS

You go through these same stages and suffer your own losses.

WHAT CAN I DO BESIDES WAIT?

You may feel controlled by the memories of what happened. You can't just forget. Even if your waking hours are relatively free of memories, you may suffer dreams or nightmares which vividly bring back the experience, sometimes making you frightened of going to sleep at all.

Give yourself permission to use every comforting tool you have ever considered or heard of, from a teddy bear in bed, to bars on the windows. Sleep is essential for your recovery. If you can find something that brings you psychological peace, don't worry about whether or not it makes rational sense. If a baseball bat by your bed is what you need, put it there.

Remember what you have enjoyed in the past and try it. Go to the ocean and throw rocks into the waves, or shout at the birds. Do you draw strength from trees or water or open spaces? Find them, and use them.

Music, art, quilts, flowers—whatever brings beauty back into your life can make a difference.

Treat yourself to every source of possible joy you can afford.(Compulsive shopping is a danger to avoid. High credit card balances will add to your anxiety.)

FOR FAMILY AND FRIENDS

Bring flowers, stuffed creatures, bright earrings, favorite foods, pretty books, a book on gardening, or sailing—there are many possibilities.

WHAT HELPS?

Depression is a normal and useful response to many situations in life. It gives time to heal before marching out and taking on new experiences. You can respond to depression in several ways. Sometimes it will disappear if you give in to it and really feel bad. Let yourself cry, be sad, mournful. If you fear giving in to the misery, create a backup. Either have a friend call "time!" for you, or be miserable in a really uncomfortable spot, such as a cold, hard kitchen chair.

Sometimes you can lift depression by talking to yourself. You have been depressed before, probably not this profoundly, but that depression passed. So will this one.

Setting yourself one task to complete each day can help you feel more in control and less depressed. Start from where you are. If you don't get dressed in the morning, start there. If you sit and stare, try reading one magazine article.

You deserve food that tastes good and is good for you. Whole unprocessed foods, fruits and vegetables, grains, help avoid sharp peaks and valleys in your moods.

Exercise can help lift depression but may be especially difficult to arrange if you fear going out alone. Walking is the simplest, easiest exercise. If you need a more secure setting, see if a local pool offers an appropriate swimming time, or if there is a local exercise class led by a knowledgeable person. Making arrangements to exercise may mean getting a baby-sitter and enlisting a friend to go with you. You deserve this step toward health.

FOR FAMILY AND FRIENDS

You have a difficult task in responding to depression. Sometimes a nudge helps, sometimes it is resented. Be willing to risk some wrong guesses about how to help.

LIFE DOESN'T FEEL WORTH THE EFFORT

If your depression begins to include obsessive thoughts of suicide or questioning the value of living, seek help. Call a crisis line. Help for depression is out there. You do not want to make a permanent decision based on a temporary feeling (although it may not feel temporary).

To reject the possibility of causing one's own death and to face instead the hard task of living with fear and of reconstructing hope, is perhaps the only truly heroic way to live.

FOR FAMILY AND FRIENDS

Although there are plenty of books to tell you otherwise, it is not always possible to see suicidal behavior as different from the depression which is a normal response to trauma. If your loved one makes a suicide attempt, know that you have been giving your best and that what creates suicidal thinking is much debated.

I CAN'T THINK ANY MORE

For many people reading is a great escape, but most victims and their families find they can't read any more. It will pass. You will be able to read, think, and talk again. If you need to read more difficult material than you can concentrate on, for work or school, challenge yourself in small degrees. Try the textbook, or technical manual or whatever it is, for a few minutes. Then go to a magazine or a lighter book.

Knowing the difficulty is normal may not help much when you burn your dinner, or shut a door on your finger, but it can lessen your sense that your mind has been stolen. It is temporary.

You can help by remembering to pay attention during tasks which ordinarly you can do unconsciously. Make lots of notes to yourself. Don't try to keep information in your head. Write it down.

FOR FAMILY AND FRIENDS

Difficulty concentrating creates trouble in school and/or at work for you also. If lowered standards won't cost you your job, try allowing yourself lowered expectations of yourself. Drop for the time being any social or community commitments which do not nourish you.

I WANT TO KILL SOMEONE

Sometimes victims feel overpowering and irrational anger toward those around them. You may feel others don't understand, or don't know what it's like. Knowing you are taking your anger out on the wrong people won't necessarily help you stop.

Your anger may be aimed clearly at the rapist, and you can't legally cause him physical harm. Some victims relieve anger by describing or imagining what would be appropriate revenge. Others feel guilty or uncomfortable at violent images. Do whichever feels right to you.

You may be able to work some of the anger out through exercise, piano playing, wood splitting, or other physical activity.

Symbolic acts, or catharsis, may generate more anger for you. Beating on a pillow might help, or it might make you feel more frustrated and wound up.

It is easy to become cynical and not expect justice. Or to become chronically bitter or angry. Those reactions take away from living. Understanding how rape happens without excusing those who perpetrate such cruelty is almost the same as holding on to two contradictory beliefs.

FOR FAMILY AND FRIENDS

You too need to be prepared for flashes of anger while driving, standing in line, or on the street. Many parents of victims report violent confrontations with strangers who are perceived to be stepping on their rights.

I THINK I NEED TO MOVE OR FIND A NEW JOB

Remember that you are vulnerable. Further change increases the stress on you. Guard your physical health:

- get rest
- don't overextend yourself
- eat well
- get moderate exercise if at all possible

Be aware that a lot of your energy is being used for healing and that your body's natural defenses are weakened. Don't enter into relationships, situations or purchases that involve your being convinced of their merit. Your sales resistance will be low.

Consider how you have coped with other losses, traumas, crises. Did that method work or make matters worse? If it helped can you find a way to use it again, now.

Many victims move within a year after an assault to feel safe again. Sometimes the change of physical surroundings helps, but not always. Sometimes people want to do everything for you, leaving you feeling helpless or vulnerable when the help stops. If someone's offers of help don't feel right, or feel overpowering, tell them you need to do things for yourself.

FOR FAMILY AND FRIENDS

You too are vulnerable and may feel the urge to make a dramatic change. Check out any serious decisions very carefully. The desire to fix things can

create a need for action, but action won't necessarily
help.

WILL I EVER FEEL BETTER ABOUT MYSELF?

Sometimes bad circumstances are made even worse by our thoughts about them. Several thoughts make recovery from an assault even harder than it already is:

It will never get better.
No one will ever care for me now.
I'm ruined (I'm not worthwhile).
My life is over.
I will never get over this.
It's the story of my life.
There is something about me which invites people to abuse me.

One way you can help yourself is to learn to counter these thoughts, in your own head or on paper. You can learn what the reasoning is behind them, and decide that you don't want to live by that reasoning any more.

Tackling these thoughts one by one is most important. When they circle in your head they are like vultures feeding on any positive feelings about yourself. On paper you can pin them down, trap them, and defuse their power.

FOR FAMILY AND FRIENDS

Check your own thoughts for predictions which make you feel worse. If you are aware of your own negative thoughts, you are in a better position to respond to hers. It is very difficult to know when to validate her feelings and when to suggest that she may feel that way, but reality could be otherwise.

IT WILL NEVER GET BETTER

The lack of consistent progress on any front, and the return of flashbacks, panic or legal action can make it seem as if you are not making progress. One word to look out for is "never." It means you are using black and white thinking, and probably aren't noticing the progress you are making. You are also predicting the future. What progress can you give yourself credit for?

Getting up in the morning
Getting dressed
Preparing meals for for yourself or others
Going shopping with someone
Going shopping alone
Completing a project at work
Starting a new project
Reading an entire magazine article
Finishing a book.

FOR FAMILY AND FRIENDS

Help her see her progress: fewer nightmares, going to school, finding a job. You can affirm her being: "I'm glad you're here." "I like the color of your hair."

NO ONE WILL EVER CARE FOR ME NOW

The fear of never finding an intimate relationship is another attempt to see into the future. Although this may feel true now, there are probably people in your life who are showing their caring as well as they can.

If it is a boyfriend you are sure you'll never have, know that many rape victims have found trustworthy supportive men to share their lives with. If you think you are ready to meet new people but never seem to, what could you do? Could you talk a friend into taking a class on being single with you? You might be able to get involved in other low pressure activities where you could meet new people without risking fear and rejection. Could you go to a local church group?

FOR FAMILY AND FRIENDS

Remember that new relationships are risky for her. Encourge her to take her time to decide about people. Continue to tell her "I care about you." "You can take as much time as you want." "I'm glad you are who you are."

I DON'T FEEL LIKE DOING ANYTHING

Part of depression is not feeling interested in anything. Part of healing is beginning activities again, even if you don't "feel" like doing anything.

Make a list of thirty things you have ever thought you might be interested in doing, and begin to work your way through them. They might include going to junk stores, an art museum, having lunch with an old friend, shopping in a new store, reading a certain book, taking a walk in the park, fixing a window box of flowers, buying yourself flowers. At first you may not feel any spark of interest. Keep at it until something clicks.

You may need to work to rediscover old interests. The assault may have robbed you of interests you held before, such as music, running, people - all may have lost their magic, or even be associated with the rape. Reclaiming those you wish to keep may mean getting a friend to participate with you, taking a local class, learning self-protection to increase your sense of safety.

Reaching out in any way to a friend, a family member or even a pet can help. Remember what brought you joy in the past: a dandelion in bloom, a puppy, the lights of the city, the smells of the market, the sounds of a department store, the sight of your children, branches against the sky, a hug from a friend. Each day look for three things which could bring you joy.

FOR FAMILY AND FRIENDS

You can remember what was enjoyed in the past and provide some help getting that started again. Do the same for yourself

SOMETIMES I FEEL SO SAD

Sadness is different from depression in that you actively mourn, cry, feel sad, grieve. It is a healthy response to loss. And a rape victim has much to grieve over. Life will never be the same. The person you were, were becoming, is not to be. (Another has taken her place.) She has to be mourned. Others may not understand your sadness. They may consider your talking about death morbid and ask you to cheer up. After all, you are alive.

Don't try to explain. Set aside a time, every week, every month, every day, when you will pay attention to your sadness, to the person you are saying good-bye to.

If you were raped when you were younger, let yourself see the paths you didn't take. And allow yourself sadness over that. It isn't necessary to dislike the life you have in order to feel sad over the one which was missed.

If you have a ritual for mourning, use it however you can.

If you fear the sadness will overtake you at times which would be embarassing—on the job, or during a social gathering—schedule a time to cry and be sad.

Even though you are sad you can know that nothing stays the same, everything changes with time. People change with experience. The new person you are is very valuable.

FOR FAMILY AND FRIENDS

Let her be sad. Know there is no "quick fix" to the grieving process. You probably need to grieve too.

SHOULD I SEE A COUNSELOR?

If you aren't making progress, feel stuck, could use a "safe" person to talk to, or think it might be useful, find help. Some rape crisis centers run groups for rape victims. Finding others who have gone through a similar experience can be a relief. The rape may also have created as a marital or family crisis you need help with.

A therapist should be knowledgeable about rape. If any therapist implies that it was somehow your fault, question him or her, and if you are not satisfied by the response, find another therapist. Sexual contact between a counselor and client is always unethical. If this comes up, leave immediately. More information about finding a therapist is in Chapter 6.

Some rape victims find they heal by helping others through the trauma of rape, or by working with others to reform the legal system to make it more responsive to victims' needs.

FOR FAMILY AND FRIENDS

It should be her decision to get counseling unless you are certain she is no longer capable of breaking out of a cycle, such as alcohol abuse or severe depression. Then you may need to find someone to assist with intervention.

If she does go to counseling, do not press for details about what is happening, but make yourself available if she wants to discuss it. You may be asked to participate depending on the circumstances. Some communities have groups for the "others" of rape victims/survivors.

5

Time Alone Doesn't Heal

It happened years ago and I can't believe after all this time I want to cry. It happened to me when I was sixteen and I didn't tell anyone. I didn't know what to call it. Will they understand if I tell them now? Is there anything I can do after all this time? How do I get started? I didn't report it. I feel terrible every time I hear about a rape. Is there more I can do?

IT HAPPENED YEARS AGO AND I CAN'T BELIEVE AFTER ALL THIS TIME I WANT TO CRY

You may be reading this book because you have remembered an incident you had overlooked, forgotten or repressed. You may find the memory remarkably fresh and painful. When rape crisis lines first began, half of their calls were from women who had never had anyone to talk to about being raped years before. They often began to cry as they related what had happened to them as childen, teenagers, or young adults.

You may find yourself stunned at the intensity of your memories. You really thought you had forgotten it, and you wonder now if you are going crazy. No. You're not. Time alone doesn't heal, although it may provide enough distance to allow you to take the steps to recover now.

While you are coping with the old pain, many of your reactions will resemble those of a recent assault victim. You may have difficulty concentrating, find yourself suddenly crying, or respond differently to your sexual partner. It is normal, and will change as you heal. You need to mourn what you now realize you lost.

FOR FAMILY AND FRIENDS

You may want to minimize the effect of someone else's past trauma on your life. It is hard to allow the disruption of your life because of something that happened before you were around.

You can be with her without travelling down the same road.

IT HAPPENED TO ME WHEN I WAS SIXTEEN AND I DIDN'T TELL ANYONE. I DIDN'T KNOW WHAT TO CALL IT

Most rape victims don't tell anyone, or tell only a friend, who may or may not help. Some told a parent who blamed them for what happened. With all the confusion about sexuality, especially in teen years it is sometimes difficult to label exploitative, manipulative, or even aggressive sexual behavior "rape." It is especially hard to name what happened as "rape" when the person is known and/or trusted.

Instead, victims often blame themselves and suffer through the following depression and anxiety without any help.

Remembering can help you understand and forgive your own behavior which was a mystery to you. Maybe you had trouble in school following a rape, or got involved with a wild crowd, or drugs and alcohol. Or maybe you were isolated, thought of yourself as different and had no friends. Part of recovery is understanding that those reactions helped you survive.

Tell someone: a friend, a counselor, a husband, a lover.

If you are hesitant about telling someone, write down what happened to you. Write it to someone as in a letter. You might address it to a friend you had at the time you didn't tell, or to a relative you think might have understood. Breaking the secrecy is the first step of beginning to break the guilt.

FOR FAMILY AND FRIENDS

Listen in the same sympathetic way you would to a recent assault.

WILL THEY UNDERSTAND IF I TELL THEM NOW?

If you were raped in the past, you still have questions of who to tell. Have you told your husband, or lover? Have you ever talked to your parents, or brothers or sisters? Do you want to now? Don't tell anyone close to you if you are unsure of the reaction until you have some support to help you.

Understanding about date rape, child sexual abuse, and rape has certainly increased, but not everyone understands that the victim is not responsible.

Recovery from past assaults is important and difficult. You deserve the support of those close to you for your courage.

FOR FAMILY AND FRIENDS

This reclaiming process can be very painful and threatening to you to live through. It may even require some change from you. It may not be fair. To be influenced so strongly by something so out of your control is frustrating. But your loved one gained some strengths which benefit you as well. Maybe remembering those can help through the difficult times.

IS THERE ANYTHING I CAN DO AFTER ALL THIS TIME?

You've already taken the first step by looking again at something painful. Many childhood traumas are now seen as having very clear and harmful effects that last into adulthood. Growing up in an alcoholic home, being abused as a child, having suffered incest, or sexual assault, add to the burden of functioning as adults.

Once you've overcome the inclination to say, "Oh that doesn't bother me any more," you may find the need to grieve, or to be angry about what happened to you. You may want to find some way to deal with the offender either symbolically or in a real confrontation. Releasing this old pain may let you live more closely to the way you want to.

You may want to enlist the help of a counselor to work your way through the process, especially if you were the victim of incest. A counselor can help you understand what promises you made to yourself when you were a child or teenager which are now standing in your way. (Guidelines for choosing a counselor are in chapter 6.) You can join a survivors' group. Working with others picking their way through the land mines laid in earlier years is a very productive way to work on recovery.

FOR FAMILY AND FRIENDS

You may struggle with your own need to minimize the harm done by an assault in the past. If she has been fine, why can't she continue to be? Her choice to work this through means she has chosen to be healthier.

HOW DO I GET STARTED?

You start by remembering what you can. Sometimes women have a sense of something happening to them when they were very young, or they have blocked the memory of what happened to them.

The search for memories shouldn't substitute for taking some of the next steps. Look at pictures of yourself as a child, and try to recapture the sense of being small, of being a child or teenager. This can trigger memories and begin to put incident(s) in perspective. You can talk to someone like a parent who might remember or confirm your suspicions. (Do not take this to mean confronting your mother if she denied what happened or blamed you for it. Confronting may or may not be useful, but it is a separate process.)

Some childhood victims' parents were supportive and can provide accurate information about the circumstances surrounding the assault.

Sometimes as in date rape, there is no one to confirm it really happened. Doubt about your memories doesn't need to stop your healing process. Although it seems like a nightmare you must have imagined because rape is so far from the reality we normally live with, if you have such flashes they probably represent memories painfully repressed.

FOR FAMILY AND FRIENDS

It is hard to review a life looking for pieces to a puzzle. She may be distant as she works on this, or talk more about her past.

I DIDN'T REPORT IT

Most children, teens and even young adults have difficulty summoning the police when they are terrified, completely confused, or threatened. Estimates of how many rapes are not reported range from three out of four to nine out of ten. There probably isn't any criminal action you can take years later, but some civil actions are filed years after an assault. An attorney can help you assess any legal action it might still be possible for you to take. There is a discussion of civil suits in the appendix.

Some states have recently passed laws which start the statute of limitations—the number of years in which legal action can take place—after recall of the incident, instead of from the time of the incident.

FOR FAMILY AND FRIENDS

Give careful thought to what actions you can support, and be honest (at least with yourself) about the energy and effort required for legal action. Carefully take stock of the resources available to you and your loved one. Draw on all those you can.

I FEEL TERRIBLE EVERY TIME I HEAR ABOUT A RAPE

You don't create anyone else's behavior. You didn't cause him to be a rapist. Reports of the criminal justice system's "revolving door" should remind you that even if you had reported the rapist, he would not necessarily have been prevented from hurting others. That thought should generate anger—not guilt—anger at a society that fails to take the issue seriously.

Sometimes listening to the news about people facing refugee camps, civil war, and constant repression, it's tempting to say "It wasn't so bad." Behavior that hurts another human, hurts. If the assaults that happen each day to women and children were reported as the political results are reported, the scale could be seen as equally "important." Minimizing one's own pain is a form of denial which stands in the way of healing.

Anger at the offender may be generated as you look at the assault with the knowledge of an adult. If the offender was in an authority position—teacher, coach, father, church youth leader—(these examples are not inclusive: within any category of people are those who use sexual violence)—anger may have been unthinkable. Now, the outrage can unload some guilt.

The best we can do for one another is break the secrecy and name the offender. Names tell others this person was real, had a family, a face, a name. He can be held responsible.

FOR FAMILY AND FRIENDS

If she has the courage to name the rapist, even though he is still in the community, maybe an important person, stand by her.

IS THERE MORE I CAN DO?

There is more you can do:

• grieving, being sad for the little girl/ young person who was hurt and didn't deserve it.

• realizing children believe bad things happen to them because they were bad, and understanding as an adult that you were not a bad child.

• forgiving yourself for anything you have been blaming yourself for, not speaking out sooner, breaking a rule, not believing it could happen again, being tricked.

• letting go of any expectations of the offender so that there is no longer a connection between you. Bitterness or resentment erodes your potential for enjoying life. This means giving up the idea that you can provide consequences or punishment while still protecting yourself (and your children).

• recognizing the lessons you learned from the assault which were inaccurate, and deciding to relearn those you choose to change:

Those close to you are going to hurt you.

You can trust people who lie to you.

You are unlovable and don't deserve to be treated well.

Sex is the only way to get love.

All men are like that.

Pleasure is shameful.

Sex is bad.

Do some of these things again and again until you really are healed.

FOR FAMILY AND FRIENDS

Depending on what type of past assault she is healing from, this will take time, patience and understanding from you. You may face some of the same shock or disillusionment you would face if she had been assaulted recently, depending on who the rapist was and what happened.

Everyone does some changing and healing from past experiences.

6

Fears, Phobias, and Persistent Problems

I can't even go outside for a walk. It's been a year, I was doing fine, now suddenly I'm re-living it. What's happening? I don't want to see people. How do I get over being afraid? I can't go to sleep without a long routine. It takes an hour. First I had nightmares of being attacked. Now I'm stabbing other people in my dreams. I'm so angry. I keep eating. I'm drinking too much. My credit cards are all at the limit and I'm still shopping. I just sit watching television. I'm afraid I'll become an abuser myself. I need to know how to pick a therapist and how to avoid being abused by one.

I CAN'T EVEN GO OUTSIDE FOR A WALK

Fear, anxiety and unpredictable panic are symptoms many victims struggle with. Studies have found that victims of rape have higher levels of fear, anxiety and phobic anxiety than nonvictims, and that these symptoms tend to be relatively persistent and long term. They can last as long as three years after the rape.

It may be that a key aspect of overcoming the negative effects of a traumatic event like rape is understanding that it is normal to develop certain problems after having been subjected to a painful, life-threatening situation. Long-term problems are not abnormal.

This means that fears of getting into a car with a man, or being afraid of going for a walk, or getting a whiff of aftershave in a shopping mall and panicking are all normal.

So what do you do about that?

Have a backup plan for the shopping trip. Ask others for help. Spread the requests for help around. Learn to say, "I frighten easily under these circumstances." Think of yourself as an accident victim with learned fears from the accident.

FOR FAMILY AND FRIENDS

Her fear is not under her control. It is beyond the fears most of us experience.

IT'S BEEN A YEAR, I WAS DOING FINE, NOW SUDDENLY I'M RELIVING IT. WHAT'S HAPPENING?

One year from the rape or sexual assault, or even twenty years later at the same time of year, you may find yourself becoming depressed or frightened for no apparent reason.

This is normal enough to have a name: "anniversary depression." Our bodies seem to have an astonishing capacity to register time, and keep track of it without our awareness. One year after a trauma, loss or death, we react again, although with less severity. It is not a setback in recovery.

You can take the opportunity to note the progress you have made toward rebuilding your life. Give yourself credit for any ability to move about: by yourself, at night, during the day. Take credit for accomplishments during the year: reading a book, finishing a project, getting a new haircut, finding another job, moving, coping from one day to the next.

If the anniversary is at a time of traditional celebration, a holiday, or spring, you may feel terribly out of step with others. Realize this won't always be true. Some year you will celebrate with others only taking note of what happened. Many who have lost a loved one during the year, or suffered rape or sexual assault, or whose family has been disrupted by the discovery of abuse, find holidays a particularly difficult time. Knowing that and taking it into account can help you plan time to mourn and acknowledge the difference between expectations and reality.

FOR FAMILY AND FRIENDS

By anticipating anniversary depression, you can be prepared instead of discouraged and surprised. Sometimes an acknowledgement and a ritual are useful; other times, simply asking if this is a hard time may be appreciated.

I DON'T WANT TO SEE PEOPLE

Sometimes the unwillingness to see people has to do with depression, but other times it is the fear of panic attacks that keeps victims at home. Smells such as aftershave, exhaust fumes, and gasoline can easily be associated with the assault, and trigger a panic attack when they are smelled later.

"Panic attacks" happen after severe loss or separation as well as after rape. They are a normal reaction to trauma. They don't make you conspicuous as a rape victim.

A panic attack is an intense burst of anxiety accompanied by marked physiological uproar and many strange changes in bodily feelings. Attacks may last from a few minutes to a few hours. The physiological uproar may include diarrhea, pounding heart, sweating palms, or general sweating, or any of the usual reactions to fright.

The fear of flashbacks or flashbacks themselves may be part of the anxiety reactions. Flashbacks are vivid pictures that replay in your head the events of the assault. They intrude into reality; that is, they can take over your awareness for a period of time. A smell is a common trigger of flashbacks, and of terror of an assault. But other events—a sound, someone who looks similar, the same kind of car—can cause the same reaction.

FOR FAMILY AND FRIENDS

You may for a time need to accompany the victim when the need to go shopping or out for any reason arises. That can be a burden.

HOW DO I GET OVER BEING AFRAID?

Some anxiety attacks may occur within a phobic situation—others not. The critical distinction between a common fear and a phobia is the degree to which it interferes with everyday life. Everyone may be afraid of going out late at night alone. But most people can do it, if they must. Someone who is phobic might would not only be unable to go out, but can panic at the thought of needing to. He or she might engage in lots of behavior to avoid that happening.

Although debate continues about the most effective treatment for phobias, some agreement exists. Psychotherapy alone is not necessarily effective in treating phobias and compulsions. Cognitive therapy focusing on what thoughts create the feelings may be useful if combined with other methods. Effective treatment for severe fears and simple phobias is systematic desensitization using controlled gradual guided exposure to things which trigger the response. You unlearn your fear by facing it one step at a time, after learning relaxation techniques.

Although you can attempt systematic desensitization on your own for low level fears, it is very difficult to do without expert help. In this case expert means someone experienced in behavior therapy and treating fears and phobias. This expert might be someone different than the person who has helped you through some of the other difficulties associated with the assault. As long as he or she is respectful of you and not exploitative, he or she doesn't need to be an expert about sexual assault.

FOR FAMILY AND FRIENDS

You may need to help her find the expert help she needs. Ask her if she would like your help making telephone calls and scheduling interviews with psychologists. She may need your encouragement to overcome the feeling that nothing can be done.

I CAN'T GO TO SLEEP WITHOUT A LONG ROUTINE. IT TAKES AN HOUR.

Compulsions may further complicate certain types of phobias. These are repetitive rituals that the sufferer feels compelled to engage in to avoid a feared consequence. Rape victims report compulsively washing for some time after the rape, to feel clean again; but the washing may take on a life of its own. Others find they have developed a time consuming routine they must complete before they can go to sleep: checking under all beds, in all closets, and the locks on all the doors and windows.

While some routine is helpful in reinstating a sense of safety, compulsions gradually undermine that sense of safety because if the routine cannot be carried out, strong anxiety results. If you can bear to stop a routine for even one night, you may break its hold. Or you may need the help of friends and family to help you avoid carrying out the routine long enough to prove to yourself that it is not what is keeping you safe.

If you can't bear to stop the routine, you need some help. Overcoming compulsions alone can be very difficult. The help of a therapist may be necessary to discover the source of these routines and determine the best treatment.

FOR FAMILY AND FRIENDS

Including spouses (partners) in therapy increases the likelihood of success.

FIRST I HAD NIGHTMARES OF BEING ATTACKED. NOW I'M STABBING OTHER PEOPLE IN MY DREAMS.

Nightmares are common. At first the dreams are a replay of the attack or the sense of powerlessness of the rape. Then as you get better the dreams may shift to generalized violence initiated by you.

Many women are horrified by the violent dreams and fear they will act out that violence. It is not a sign that you are going to be violent because you are having violent dreams. No matter what you may think about dreams as symbolic or prophesy, the violence in the dreams is an attempt to make sense somehow of what happened. The most positive way to view them is as an effort to reclaim your power. Some victims report a final dream in which they are able to defeat the rapist. Often the general fear in their lives is reduced after that.

FOR FAMILY AND FRIENDS

Reassure her that you don't think she is going to go out and knife someone or shoot people. There is a difference between feelings, dreams and action.

I'M SO ANGRY

It may feel like anger is taking over your life. You may find yourself angry at those close to you for little or no reason. You may find yourself just irrationally angry all the time. You may be angry with God that He allowed this to happen to you, or with someone who didn't protect you: your mother, a boy friend, husband, lover. You can release some of this anger by:

- splitting wood
- throwing rocks into the ocean
- shouting in your car, or where others can't hear you
- hitting a pillow
- writing it all down describing the anger, or describing those who hurt you in the most evil terms
- telling a friend, a support group
- talking to a counselor who is comfortable with anger
- drawing the anger on a piece of paper and ripping it up
- focusing it on a piece of life which needs changing and needs your energy to do it.

FOR FAMILY AND FRIENDS

You have two tasks: to handle your own anger without damage to yourself or the victim, and to avoid taking her anger as a personal attack. With so much free floating anger some of it gets misdirected in response to very trivial behaviors.

I KEEP EATING

Difficulty with eating patterns is a common symptom for assault victims of all ages. Some have trouble eating after an assault, then develop further difficulties. Or because so many people turn to food to fill other needs, overeating becomes a difficulty.

Eating for comfort, eating because it is the only thing that brings pleasure, eating unconsciously out of boredom are all patterns that can persist. Sometimes people eat to develop fat for protection from others.

If you have also lost your exercise habits, it is even more difficult to turn the cycle around. Eating habits have been the subject of too many books already, but some things are worth repeating.

Starvation diets don't work, and worse, train the body to get by on less food. Finding other ways to take care of yourself is probably the best strategy for managing food issues. Make a list for yourself of other things you can do besides eating to feel better: call a friend, go outside, take a bubble bath, take a walk. Support groups can be helpful, especially those which acknowledge the many issues involved in eating.

FOR FAMILY AND FRIENDS

Try to stay out of the food issue. Reassurance about continued caring may help, or may not. Requests for weight loss may only increase her sense of being out of control.

I'M DRINKING TOO MUCH

Alcohol is an easy drug to reach for. The numbness it provides can be welcome relief. But the price is high. If you are mixing alcohol and other drugs for sleep or anxiety, you need help finding alternative methods of coping.

Some doctors, especially those unwilling or unprepared to cope with the crisis of rape, are too ready to prescribe tranquilizers or sleeping pills. Friends may be too ready to get you drinking to forget pain. Numbing out for a time may not be bad as long as you know healing isn't going on, and that alcohol can contribute significantly to depression and sleep disturbances. You may become worried about your own use of alcohol, or those around you may become concerned, adding to your sense of being out of control.

If you are worried about your alcohol use and you don't know much about the disease of alcoholism, find a *knowledgeable* substance abuse counselor to discuss your concerns with.

FOR FAMILY AND FRIENDS

If she is drinking too much, you may need to intervene. First learn what you can about codependency—the way others around a substance-abusing person contribute to the addiction—so you won't make matters worse. Learn what you need to about intervention. There are programs to assist families in which drug problems occur. If you are drinking to blunt your own emotions, set yourself a deadline and a contract for finding other methods of relieving the tension and feeling better (or less awful).

MY CREDIT CARDS ARE ALL AT THE LIMIT AND I'M STILL SHOPPING

All coping methods have their place, and certainly shopping is one way of looking for a lift. Advertising promises of new selves and lives can suck us into feeling like one more new pair of shoes, or one perfect dress, will give us the lift we need.

But if the credit card payment anxiety increases past the pleasure gained, it is past time to reconsider. We hope you read this first and recognize compulsive shopping in time to look for another way to take care of yourself.

FOR FAMILY AND FRIENDS

If you can recognize the needs she is trying to fill with shopping, you can help find other ways to meet those needs. Some new clothes or changes to a room can decrease old associations, and produce some positive feelings. But they are a tool, not a solution.

I JUST SIT WATCHING TELEVISION

Watching hours and hours of television is another coping method that can create new problems, and stop your progress toward recovery. As entertainment or a way to pass the time, it has its place, but it can become a handy method of avoiding change.

FOR FAMILY AND FRIENDS

You can express your concern about endless hours of television, and offer your company for other activities.

I'M AFRAID I'LL BECOME AN ABUSER MYSELF

You may experience some fears because of what you have seen on television, read in the newspaper, or heard from others about what happens to rape or sexual abuse victims. Statements range from "Children of sexual abuse victims are more likely to be abused" to "We know why she is the way she is. It's because she was raped."

Some statements are based on totally mistaken ideas, and some reflect statistical trends that need not be true for you. Remember that almost all of them are based on a time before help was available to victims of sexual violence. By getting help, you will rebuild the life you want.

FOR FAMILY AND FRIENDS

You too may fear the future. Marriages fall apart, individuals lose their jobs, or drop out of school. There is no denying the enormous destructive potential of sexual violence. But fortune telling—attempting to predict the future—is totally wasted effort, other than anticipating a time when the pain will lessen.

I NEED TO KNOW HOW TO PICK A THERAPIST AND HOW TO AVOID BEING ABUSED BY ONE.

Finding a counselor you like and trust will probably take some work. Ask your friends and family members if they know anyone. The local rape crisis center may have referrals they can give you. But no matter what the source, *you* are the one who must establish a working relationship. The counselor who was just right for your best friend's relationship problems may not be the right one for you.

You can make appointments with more than one counselor and interview them all. They are working for you.

1. Interview therapists to find out what method of treatment they use and what they know about sexual assault. Sometimes generalists can be helpful, but sometimes they have their own crises when presented with the reality of rape. You don't need their issues on top of your own. Someone who doesn't have specific knowledge of the rape trauma syndrome, or post traumatic stress disorder, may underestimate or not recognize the source of some of your symptoms.

2. If you have specific problems such as phobias, eating disorders or alcohol abuse you want to work on, be sure the counselor has experience in those particular areas. Each has optimal methods of treatment.

3. Ask for some guidelines about the length of time the therapist expects you to be in treatment. If she or he is not willing to give you an estimate, find another therapist. You may need long term therapy,

but open ended treatment tends to be less productive.

4. Once you begin with a counselor knowing when to quit is tough. If you don't feel respected, valued, or understood, or if your experience is minimized or distorted, it's a sign you haven't found the right person. If a counselor suggests sexual contact would be helpful, terminate therapy immediately. Sexual contact between counselor and client is prohibited by the ethical code of every type of counselor, psychologist, and social worker.

5. Money is a real issue when it comes to treatment. Most therapists will be straightforward about costs and some offer sliding fees. Some states have Victim Compensation programs which will pay some of the costs. Medical insurance sometimes will pay for counseling and some companies have employee assistance programs which may pay for mental health services.

6. Counseling is not always comfortable, and for a while you could feel more unsettled. You will know you've found good counseling when you develop more and more skills to help yourself as time goes on. You become able to recognize your own patterns and interpret your own emotions. And you will develop healthier methods of responding to those patterns and emotions.

7

Finding Pleasure Again

No one talks about sex. I keep hearing rape is a violent crime and not a sexual one. Sometimes when I try to make love, I feel like I'm right back in the rape again. I don't want to hurt my partner anymore, but I can't help it. This has opened old wounds. I want to make love but my partner doesn't want anything to do with me. Guilt gets in the way. I seem to be taking too many risks. What's going on? What about AIDS? I hate my body. It feels soiled, damaged.

NO ONE TALKS ABOUT SEX

The sexual response is affected by nearly all stress, certainly by rape. Sexuality and desire are fragile and complex under normal circumstances. It is no wonder that flashbacks, fear, terror or loss of self-esteem make sex difficult for a time.

You may experience any one of the reactions rape victims talk about. You may want sex right away with a loving partner to reassure yourselves you are normal. You may feel no desire.

You may know you want to abstain for weeks. You may want to have sex, but find you experience flashbacks. Flashbacks may be triggered by any sexual stimulation, including masturbation.

You will probably be frustrated with how slowly you heal, and how out of control your body feels. Your comfort level may change from day to day— even hour to hour. What was comfortable yesterday may be frightening today.

You may be frightened of all men and feel distaste, fright, or even a physical reaction such as vomiting, at the thought of sexual contact.

You might respond to degradation or loss of virginity with risk taking behavior that feels out of your control.

The problems you face will depend on whether you are attached to someone at the time of the rape, what the circumstances of the rape were—for example, whether it was a stranger or a date—and what support and help you receive from your partner, friends and acquaintances.

FOR FAMILY AND FRIENDS

You can't predict what your partner will want or need. So much of what affects sexual behavior is not understood. You will need to ask, be prepared to be rejected and understand her response may have little to do with you.

Support her right to set her own pace. Reassure her that she is lovable. If you are family or friend, avoid statements about her behavior which can sound judgemental even if you disagree with sexual choices she is making.

I KEEP HEARING RAPE IS A VIOLENT CRIME AND NOT A SEXUAL ONE

Most people understand that rape is not a sexual experience in the way sex is supposed to be—with mutual consent between adults—but is rather an act of power and violence. It is closer to being mugged or robbed at gun point.

The motivation of the rapist doesn't seem to matter to the body's response to the violence. It creates sexual difficulties not taken care of simply by calling rape "violent." Maybe you're confused about how to label what happened because you were victimized in a dating or party situation and it didn't feel "violent." Maybe you were interested in eventual sexual activity with the person who raped you. Maybe you are/were married to him. It is rape, anytime you don't have a choice.

Some victims cut themselves off from their sexuality because of the links to the terror and violence of the rape. The goal is to reclaim your body for yourself. Someone else took control of your body and used it without your consent (even if you submitted).

If you don't have a partner, you may choose to avoid sexual relationships for a time. If you have a partner, you still may want to avoid sex for a time. Sex is such a core issue in relationships, you will need to judge what you can ask for. If you can, let your partner know how you are feeling. Ask for the time and the chance to set your own pace; to be in control of what happens sexually. Or ask for some particular changes to help you feel safer: a light on, perhaps, or a change in positions.

FOR FAMILY AND FRIENDS

The fabric of her being has been torn by the attack. She may need to mend before any vulnerability is safe for her. What feels like sexual rejection is very threatening, but she has little control over this response.

SOMETIMES WHEN I TRY TO MAKE LOVE, I FEEL LIKE I'M RIGHT BACK IN THE RAPE AGAIN.

To trust another, and to regain intimacy, you need to feel secure about your ability to protect yourself. As closeness increases, so does the sense of vulnerability. That can trigger anxiety, which might block sexual feelings.

Anything you can say to your partner will help him (or her). He is as bewildered as you about how to respond and probably wants to help but doesn't know how. If he continues to ask about sex, will you feel pressured? If he doesn't will you feel rejected? And often the answer to both is, "yes." If he knows that, he may feel more comfortable using his own feelings as a guide, taking some of the pressure off of you.

Fear and risk heighten sexual feelings for some people. If the fear is not overwhelming and you are in a genuinely safe place, reassurance from your partner might let you move through the fear instead of stopping and letting it control you.

If your communication and assertiveness skills were good before the rape, you already have the tools to establish the guidelines you need. If you are like most people, you didn't talk much about sex or touching before the assault and this is a particularly difficult time to begin. But relying on unspoken agreements or signals probably won't work very well.

FOR FAMILY AND FRIENDS

Ask, be gentle, patient. And take care of yourself. Play handball, run, or work out, to keep yourself feeling okay.

I DON'T WANT TO HURT MY PARTNER ANYMORE, BUT I CAN'T HELP IT.

Your partner's reaction is critical to how well you do during this time, but both of you need to know there will be times when no matter what your partner does, it will be wrong. Conflicting needs for comfort and distance, reassurance and fear of dependency mean that sometimes there is no right way. You may want to feel attractive to your partner, but not want to be pressured. You may want him to make the approaches, but not want to have to say "no" when you aren't ready. You may want your partner to read your mind. (Don't we always.)

Your partner is likely to be surprised and hurt when he realizes that sometimes things he does trigger flashbacks. Lesbian partners are upset to find that they are not immune to sexual problems.

You can help by suggesting other ways your partner can show caring: talking with you, listening, comforting you, buying you an ice cream cone, flowers, or taking you to a movie.

If you want physical contact, and aren't sure what sexual contact is going to be okay, suggesting some ways to have physical contact will help both of you feel more in control. Are hugs okay? Kisses, massage, holding hands, sitting close together, a neck rub? If you know you don't want to be touched on your breasts or genitals, tell your partner that isn't going to work for a while.

If you are open to sexual contact you may still find that smells, behaviors, words, touches or looks can trigger fear, anxiety, or flashbacks. You need to be able to stop the sexual activity if you want to. Set up an agreement with your partner about how that will happen. Can you just say, "Stop, I'm having trouble," or do you need a signal too?

It should not be surprising if both you and your partner find all this disturbing and frustrating. To have the rapist(s) intrude in your most loving moments with a partner is painful.

FOR FAMILY AND FRIENDS

Many couples have unspoken agreements about sex and when those arrangements are disturbed, both feel insecure and afraid of what might happen to the relationship. Difficult as it may be, try to remember what an important person you are to her, and how crucial you are to her recovery.

THIS HAS OPENED OLD WOUNDS

If you were assaulted during your childhood, you may find this assault triggers those feelings too. This may be the time to find a therapist. (See chapter 6 about choosing a counselor.)

A counselor can help you decide what problems to tackle first. When new problems retrigger old, the overload can stop you totally.

FOR FAMILY AND FRIENDS

This is time for help. Even the most supportive family and friends can only do just so much. And sometimes your trust is stretched when you hear that someone was assaulted before. But this is very common. There are estimates that as many as one in two child victims of abuse are victimized again as adults.

I WANT TO MAKE LOVE BUT MY PARTNER DOESN'T WANT ANYTHING TO DO WITH ME.

Maybe the most difficult reaction for you is if your partner appears to be angry with you, rejects your advances or appears to have no interest in sexual contact with you. Although you may be tempted to guess why he is reacting this way, it's best to ask. He may be extremely angry with the rapist, which interferes with his sexual interest. He may want to give you the room to feel comfortable and not want to pressure you. He may feel guilty for some part he feels he played in the assault (not having fixed the car or picked you up on time, leaving you at a party, not fixing a lock, or introducing him to you). Or he may be feeling the more traditional feelings of betrayal and contamination. If this last is the case, he may feel guilty about it and not want to reveal it, or not know what to do.

Just as you have no direct outlet for your anger, neither does he. In your frustration, both of you may end up angry with each other.

FOR FAMILY AND FRIENDS

You may not want to feel threatened, but may. You may not want to see your partner as contaminated, or unfaithful, but may. You may not want to feel angry at her for "letting it happen" but may. As much as you can, you need to be responsible for those issues yourself, maybe seeking some outside help. Don't ask your partner to reassure or "help" you with these.

GUILT GETS IN THE WAY

Guilt over what happened leading up to the rape or during the rape may be interfering with your desire to resume sexual contact with a partner. Sometimes rapes occur after a fight with a partner, alcohol use, or flirting. Then when the rape happens, it may look like unfaithfulness.

Someone who fantasized about rape before a rape may feel confused about what she did want. Rape fantasies are erotic because the person fantasizing has control over an out of control situation. Rape is never anything like a rape fantasy for the victim. Pornography makes this more confusing, because it often portrays women liking the degradation of rape.

You may feel even more guilty and confused if your body responded. Orgasm has been known to occur in extreme, even life threatening situations. Fear or terror creates a high level of excitement in the body, and with suffcient physical pressure, orgasm can happen automatically. That doesn't mean the victim liked or enjoyed what happened or had any sexual feelings during the assault. Trying to understand, or explaining that to a partner, can be impossible.

Sometimes people feel less guilty and secretive by writing what they can't say aloud in a letter to their partner, knowing they are not going to give it to them. Do not give in to the urgings of your partner to tell what happened in the assault. It would only create images that will come between you. It doesn't explain anything.

FOR FAMILY AND FRIENDS

Allow your partner privacy about the details of the assault. Most rape victims feel their life is at stake and often are forced to submit to acts they would never consider in a loving relationship. Do not misinterpret submission to terror for anything else.

I SEEMS TO BE TAKING TOO MANY RISKS. WHAT'S GOING ON?

Some victims repeat risky experiences in what may be an effort to get control over the experience. This reaction can happen for a variety of reasons. A sexual barrier of virginity may have been broken, and either the woman feels of little value, or with the barrier broken there is no reason not to engage in sexual activity. Maybe it is a compulsive repetition with the hope of finding pleasure and caring. Maybe an inability to set limits, to say "no" to people, allows situations to develop she feels she can't get out of. These actions suggest the need for help to avoid further victimization.

Finding help or turning to a friend can be very difficult because of the stigma attached to female sexual activity. "Promiscuity" is an easily attached judgement most women still fear. But working through the pain of being a rape victim may seem even harder.

The most likely place to find help is through a women's clinic, family planning or social service center that supports women's rights to choose sexual activity based on their own needs.

FOR FAMILY AND FRIENDS

As a friend or family member, avoid attaching judgements to her behavior. You may have good reason to be concerned, but she can only hear that concern if it is not attached to traditional labels.

WHAT ABOUT AIDS?

Much is still unknown about AIDS and its transmission. Cases of transmittal with one sexual contact from male to female have been documented. A University of California study found the likelihood of infection from having vaginal intercourse once with an infected partner without using a condom to be one in 500.

Because rape often involves other forms of sexual contact a better predictor may be whether the rapist comes from a high-risk group. When the rapist is known, you may want him tested for AIDS. However, legal restrictions around the release of such information may make that useless. In the case of an unknown, never arrested rapist, you can only guess about the risk.

The chances are very low that you would develop AIDS but you may want to be tested for the AIDS antibody at the recommended intervals for a period of time. A knowledgeable clinic such as your local Public Health department can help you make those choices, and provide reassurance about the relative likelihood of developing AIDS.

FOR FAMILY AND FRIENDS

It may be hard to be patient, forgiving or hopeful in the face of fear of AIDS. Learn as much as you can about it so you can make your own assessment of risk. You may want to consider practicing safe sex for a time. Figure out how to set the fear aside, as you do other fears–earthquakes, nuclear holocaust, automobile accidents, cancer. You live with all these everyday. AIDS is really just one more.

I HATE MY BODY. IT FEELS SOILED, DAMAGED

During the sexual assault, control was taken away.

Taking back control of your body means feeling good about your body again, setting limits and finding ways to find comfort, nurturance, pleasure and intimacy again.

Rituals or procedures can help.

Sometimes going to a doctor, or a clinic or a women's health center can reassure you that you are intact and healthy.

Doing something outdoors—hiking, swimming in the ocean—helps some people feel healthy again.

Can you think of a purification ritual that would make you feel better?

You may find some exercises for learning about your own body helpful, if they are not too threatening. Looking at yourself in the mirror without clothes and enjoying your strength and positive features can be a step.

You can notice ways your body works that bring you pleasure: walking easily, playing sports, nurturing a child, seeing a sunset, hearing music, reading a book.

FOR FAMILY AND FRIENDS

Appreciate her smile, her caring, her efforts to be present. Tell her you're glad she is alive and that she is courageous to struggle with the effects.

8

Cracks in the Cosmos

I believed if I was a good person, people would be good to me. I don't want to look at everyone with suspicion. Is God punishing me? Am I ruined? My religion requires forgiveness. Letting go is surprisingly hard. How can I forgive those who let me down? How can I forgive myself? How do I make sense of this?

I BELIEVED IF I WAS A GOOD PERSON, PEOPLE WOULD BE GOOD TO ME

Rape shatters assumptions about the world and the self. It shatters the assumption of personal invulnerabilty, the sense that although people get hurt in automobile accidents, it won't happen to me. Or if I just follow the rules of safe conduct, I'll be safe.

It shatters the sense of meaningfulness in the world. Beliefs that if you are a good person, good things will happen to you no longer make sense. Instead of losing this belief, people search for meaning in the victimization. Sometimes this leads to notions such as "God is punishing me for wrongdoing."

It shatters self-esteem.

People are unaware of these assumptions until something traumatic forces them to recognize and examine them. People minimize their own victimization to lessen the threat to their assumptions.

Rebuilding assumptions that give the world meaning is an intensely personal task. It involves coming to terms with a world in which bad things can and do happen to oneself.

FOR FAMILY AND FRIENDS

Your assumptions have also been shattered. The sense of vulnerablity can be very frightening. Recognize you may want to rush into new beliefs to lessen anxiety, but that they may involve harmful, limiting assumptions about security such as "The world is out to get anyone who trusts someone else."

I DON'T WANT TO LOOK AT EVERYONE WITH SUSPICION

One choice is to decide the world is an intensely dangerous place and that you will change your behavior accordingly. Maybe you think you were too naive and trusting, and are going to resolve to trust no one.

That is one way to gain some control. Another is to decide to live on the edge and court danger, try to find the edge of safety. This isn't recommended, but recognizing it as a strategy may help you understand what you are trying to do.

Another is seeing the cracks in the cosmos, but letting down your guard anyway to be fully open to life's possibilities. It is living with the knowledge of vulnerability and fragility in all of life. Choosing a conscious vulnerability can allow for increased pleasure in life, but it takes time and practice to achieve.

FOR FAMILY AND FRIENDS

Recognize that differences of perception about how dangerous the world is are not objectively arguable. You can state that you see an activity, action, or situation as dangerous, or relatively safe; but don't assume your partner, or child, can take your word for it. Agree to see the world differently when you can. Sometimes you will need to argue about your needs for safety, having doors locked, or a car parked safely.

IS GOD PUNISHING ME?

No one is uniquely vulnerable to other humans living outside the rules. It seems sacriligious to see rapists as instruments of God. No matter what sin a woman or child has committed, rape is not a punishment a just, loving god would provide.

Blaming yourself, or God, for the violence may, for a time, help give meaning to an event which makes no sense, for which there is no good reason.

The human spirit's resiliency is sorely tested by sexual violence. That testing can be turned into your future strength, but that doesn't justify in any way the original violence that led to the testing.

FOR FAMILY AND FRIENDS

Understand the questioning as a part of trying to make sense of the world again. Try to avoid judging her on the basis of the loss of faith. If you know someone within your religious community who can be trusted not to blame the victim, or require forgiveness, you might suggest she talk to that person about faith and what it means. To be deprived of the faith which made the world make sense is a real loss.

AM I RUINED?

Cultures that believe a woman is ruined if she has sexual intercourse outside of marriage, and include rape, complicate the recovery process.

If you are part of a culture that believes this, you will need to challenge your own belief. To make peace with your culture you might want to move outside it, or change it, or find other members who disagree within it. Organizations such as the Center for the Prevention of Sexual and Domestic Violence in Seattle, or a local rape crisis center may be able to identify others working for change within religious communities.

A human being is never worthless. The issue is one of choice. To believe a human is ruined by another's violence is to underestimate the strength- and source-of human dignity.

Part of the intent of the statement, "Rape is a violent crime, not a sexual crime," is to remove some of the stigma from the victim. It means that the rapist is not responding to sexual signals from the victim and the victim should not be held accountable for the sexual form of the attack. The concept of psychological virginity might be helpful to you if you are not yet married. It says that you are still a virgin until you decide to give away your virginity.

FOR FAMILY AND FRIENDS

If you hold cultural beliefs that a woman's worth is linked to her "purity" you will need to overcome them. Women's bodies are no more "contaminated" by sexual contact then are men's.

MY RELIGION REQUIRES FORGIVENESS

The Random House dictionary defines "forgive" as "to renounce anger or resentment against; to cease to feel hostility, resentment or hatred for."

In a societal sense rapists should never be forgiven. For too many years rapists (unless they were black) raped without consequence. Even after twenty years of reform, some types of rape—date or workplace rape—continue to go unpunished by the law.

The suggestion that rapists be forgiven can also imply that the woman raped, not the rapist, is responsible. Rapists are held too little accountable already, so why suggest forgiveness?

Forgiveness is only useful to you for one purpose: to break the connection between you and the person who assaulted you. The desire for revenge, justice, or to be the instrument of his punishment, takes energy from you. You need the energy for yourself and relationships that nurture you. Feelings of resentment erode the joy of living.

The goal is to let go of the connection without blaming yourself, becoming cynical, or excusing the rapist.

FOR FAMILY AND FRIENDS

You feel your connection to the rapist when you scan faces for him. Or avoid stores, or neighborhoods where you know he might be because you are still afraid of your reaction. Your task, too, is to lessen the control he has on your life.

LETTING GO IS SURPRISINGLY HARD

A search for forgiveness should not be allowed to short circuit your healing. You'll probably need to go through some difficult emotions before you've reached the stage of letting go. To let go, you need a certain detachment (not to be confused with denial or minimization of the harm done you).

Letting go means being able to think coolly of that person, without your stomach knotting up, and without your mind racing off into tight circles of how he can be hurt.

Forgiveness can give serenity. Or, maybe, you have to reach a level of serenity to forgive. If you can realize the other person has his own path to follow and his own lessons to learn in life, you may be able to relinquish the personal need to hand him the consequences, to punish him. Not all injustices can be fixed. It takes humility to know what is possible.

It is helpful to believe in a creative force in the universe—God, Goddess—to have a way to nurture your spiritual side.

Forgiveness can feel strange. By not forgiving people, you keep a strong connection.

It is hard to forgive when you are the one paying the price in money, emotional pain, and missed opportunities.

FOR FAMILY AND FRIENDS

Forgiving should not be pushed. Anger, desire for revenge, and dreams of violence all come before the process of distancing can even begin. For both you and the survivor.

HOW CAN I FORGIVE THOSE WHO LET ME DOWN?

Forgiveness can be of different types. Some people close to you may have reacted very badly. You may want to continue a relationship with some, and let others go. Your husband may have said hurtful things, your mother blamed you, your friends left you alone. You may be able to excuse some people through an awareness that they reacted out of their own guilt, fear or ignorance. They may have apologized for their inablity to act.

Others may continue to ignore your pain, or even blame you for what happened. Your task is to let go of expectations of those who aren't going to change, and forgive those you want to be close to.

That requires a different kind of forgiveness or acceptance than letting go does. Opening up your heart to that person, to feel warmth, to be willing to be vulnerable again, is emotional forgiveness.

Only those who show good will in changing, who can say "Yes I wronged you, I regret that," deserve your emotional forgiveness. Your continuing forgiveness can be based on the other's actions to follow through on changes.

You never want to open up your heart to further abuse.

FOR FAMILY AND FRIENDS

If there are actions you regret, apologize. If you have added to her burden, what can you DO now to help? Words are not enough.

You may need to forgive those who let you down, too.

HOW CAN I FORGIVE MYSELF?

Blaming yourself for some action you did or didn't take during the assault is a natural way to maintain some control. Eventually, though, you need to forgive yourself.

That process may be more difficult if you did anything which you think contributed to the assault. If you were drinking, using drugs or were in a place you considered dangerous, you may find it more difficult to forgive yourself.

Your recovery depends on moving from blaming something essential about yourself—being a bad judge of character or a bad person—to deciding that no matter how you judge the choices you made, you didn't make the assault happen.

If you are having trouble forgiving your own powerlessness in the situation, you may gain some comfort by remembering that while you can be helpless in preventing the attack you are *not* helpless in the recovery process. You can be powerless, and powerful in coping with it.

If you believe we create our own reality, you may be searching for the rapist's purpose in your life. Forgiving yourself may mean recognizing that the intersection of lives may not have had to do with your life, but with the rapist's.

While remembering that the blame lies with the rapist, you can say to yourself, "I forgive myself." You can ask a higher power for forgiveness. You can ask others to forgive you. You can acknowledge to yourself what you wish you had done differently

FOR FAMILY AND FRIENDS

Understand the difference between believing this happened because the victim was a bad person, and the desire on her part to feel more in control by judging some of her own behavior.

Your reassurances that you blame the rapist, not her, for what happened may be very helpful.

HOW DO I MAKE SENSE OF THIS?

Life can be seen as a series of lessons, rather than a test. Hardships provide opportunity for growth into light and clarity, or into hardness and sterility. No one would choose the opportunity, certainly. But you can reclaim your life. Your life is yours to live again.

One woman said, "I took my life, my safety, my security for granted before I was raped (a year ago today). Now I am grateful for every day I live. I see things I never saw before."

The journey to this spot is long, and it is not a journey anyone should be forced to take. Even reaching this place of rejoicing in each day does not dissolve the cruelty of rape. But the choice to stay the same has been taken away from you. Now you can only make of it what you can.

FOR FAMILY AND FRIENDS

The choice to grow and change in response to hardship is individual. No one can hurry someone into acceptance of what has happened and a healthier response. You can help; you can't hurry.

9

Are All Men Rapists?

Are all men rapists? How can they do it? His friends and family defend him. How can they? Why would anyone want to do that to someone else? Are they crazy? What goes on in their heads? Will he rape again? What happens to him if he is caught? Will he come back? Does everyone who is abused become an abuser? Can I trust anyone? I still don't understand.

ARE ALL MEN RAPISTS?

No. Not all men are rapists. Even in the surveys in which many men give pro-rape answers, twelve percent say that under no circumstances is it okay to use force to gain sexual intercourse. Other studies confirm that a large number of men find the use of force horrifying and don't understand how others can use it.

Who you mistrust now will be determined by a number of factors. Was the assailant known to you, trusted, or a stranger? Was he young, or did he use an age difference to establish trust or authority over you and then take advantage of that? Did he inflict injuries in addition to the sexual assault, or did he yell obscenities, or imply that you really wanted it? Was he drinking? Was he from the same racial group or another-an oppressor group, or an oppressed group?

Many women find they are frightened of men who resemble the rapist in body type, or racial group. But not all men of any group are rapists.

FOR FAMILY AND FRIENDS

Her fears may not make any sense to you. If you can remind yourself they are not under her control it may help you be more patient. Don't settle for racial stereotypes as an explanation for rape.

HOW CAN THEY DO IT?

No one knows for sure why rape happens. The theories are as different as the ways in which people study rapists. Some people see attackers as troubled in some way, as "psychopathological." They look for reasons: "They were abused as children themselves, their mothers were cold and distant, their fathers were cold and distant, they grew up with violence."

Others see society as causing the problem. Rape is shown in movies, magazines and television as acceptable, sometimes even erotic. Some see the way boys are raised to push for sex, and girls to resist advances, as a setup for rape.

Some people have suggested that addiction is a way to understand rape. They see a sex offender as addicted to the excitement and release that a rape creates for him.

The role of alcohol in rape is debated, but half to two-thirds of all rapes involve the use of alcohol. An individual man may use alcohol to give himself permission to do something he would not otherwise do; in gangs it serves as glue.

Gang rape is more common than previously supposed. Even "nice" guys can be involved through alcohol, pressure from others, and a fear of being less than masculine. If you were a victim of gang rape the gap between how you see the rapists and how their friends and family see them may be even greater and more horrifying than in other cases.

FOR FAMILY AND FRIENDS

Sometimes you may feel blamed or accused by the victim's mistrust of men, and her anger at them. If she begins to understand what happened to her as part of a larger picture, you may be asked to make some changes.

HIS FRIENDS AND FAMILY DEFEND HIM. HOW CAN THEY?

It is shocking to realize that a rapist usually has friends, a girlfriend or a wife, parents, grandparents, and others who are certain he couldn't have done such a thing. They know who rapists are: they are part of another racial group, they look the part of a bad person, and nobody could love them. Their son, lover, friend, isn't like that, so you must be mistaken. But you know you're not.

Denial is part of the dynamic around sexual violence. It is extremely difficult to come to terms with the reality that someone loved can commit such a crime.

People have an amazing ability to ignore, distort and forget things they have done, seen, or heard. When they deny they were involved in a rape, their minds may really protect them from the memory of how they behaved. Rapists see victims as willing, or deserving. (Denial is extremely powerful because it operates without any awareness that something is being forgotten or ignored.)

FOR FAMILY AND FRIENDS

If you must confront the rapist's family because of a trial or because you live in the same community, your anger at them may be stronger than at the rapist. Unable to grasp how he could behave as he does, the mind goes for something easier—a family doing wrong and not knowing it.

WHY WOULD ANYONE WANT TO DO THAT TO SOMEONE ELSE?

While you struggle to understand what happened to you, you will probably hear that a rapist rapes for power, not for sex.

If that idea is useful to you, you have plenty of support for keeping it. If it isn't, or doesn't make sense to you, you have support too. The reality seems to be that some rapists rape primarily for power, while others use only as much force as they need to achieve their sexual ends. Does it matter? What happened to you was damaging, destructive, and hurtful regardless of the rapist's motivation.

Trying to understand the rapist is part of the need to make sense of your own victimization. If you could just understand why he did it, maybe you would understand why it happened to you.

FOR FAMILY AND FRIENDS

The urge to understand is the human drive to make sense of events. To make sense of rape is impossible, because it is not an act based on sense, reason, or rationality. Even if you find an answer for yourself about who the rapist is, or why he did what he did, remember your answer may not bring your loved one any comfort. Be careful of imposing the answer which has brought you peace on anyone else.

ARE THEY CRAZY?

Some people would argue that to do what a rapist does, he must be crazy. If it is easier to think of him as crazy, that's okay, as long as you realize that the legal or mental health system may not see him that way.

This idea that a sex offender is crazy is used against women who accuse men of assaulting them or their children, if no evidence of craziness is found. The logic is: rapists are crazy, this man is not crazy, therefore he couldn't possibly be a rapist. People want to believe that normal people couldn't do such a thing in order to protect their own sense of security.

FOR FAMILY AND FRIENDS

It may be harder to believe what you are told about the victimization if you know the offender, and know he isn't crazy and believe that a rapist must be crazy. But what person trusts someone who shows any signs of being crazy? The lack of any "craziness" that shows is precisely how many rapists operate.

WHAT GOES ON IN THEIR HEADS?

A sex offender treatment specialist gave the following testimony about rapists during a Seattle trial about a party gang rape. As a clinical psychologist he specializes in evaluation and treatment of sexual offenders. He was at the trial to talk about men who could gang rape and then lie about it in the courtroom with no signs of embarassment, humiliation, or remorsefulness.

Q. "How can they do it? How can somebody rape somebody and then believe he didn't cause any harm?"

A. "Basically, when a person engages in some kind of non-consenting sexual relations, two things are occurring. On the one hand, the person is experiencing some kind of sexual arousal. It feels good. On the other hand, there's most likely a perception at some level that the behavior is inappropriate. That creates internal conflict that a person needs to resolve.

"Generally, people resolve that conflict by ... creating a fantasy in their mind as to what the activity actually was. Part of the fantasy are justifications like, 'The person was willing to do it, she (or he) deserved it, there wasn't any harm, I didn't really do it.' So, typically, what you see is a variety of distortions around the rape experience. That the victims enjoyed it, that they asked for it, that they were consenting in some fashion, or that their reputation was such that they deserved what took place.

"Essentially people reconstruct the situation so that they no longer experience any internal discomfort regarding what they did. That allows them in many instances to repeat and to escalate, as the situation then becomes essentially justified in their own thinking.

"A rapist does this so he can live with himself and think of himself as a normal person. Most people like to think of themselves in good terms. And in any kind of situation in which non-consenting sexual relations occur, the person has to distort the experience in some fashion. The attacker either convinces himself that no harm was done, or that the victim had it coming, or that his action was justified in some other fashion."

Q. "To what extent would a rapist go to rationalize or justify or try to make himself look good?"

A. "He will describe incidents that other observers and participants in a situation simply don't report. "

Q. "Do you find that rapists tend to have inadequate social skills? "

A. "Many rapists in fact have very good superficial social skills. It's generally the clinical consensus, as well as what has come out of research, though, that people who engage in rape behavior tend to have concerns about their personal adequacy. They suffer feelings of insecurity, and doubt their basic masculine adequacy. They defend themselves in ways that are generally very rigid, utilizing a great deal of denial."

Q. "Do rapists tend to be manipulative and use people?"

A. "In general, yes. You often do see a person who manipulates people, who uses persons for their own ends."

Q. "How about preying on vulnerable people?"

A. "That happens. You see a variety of circumstances and methods that people use to pick out their victims."

Q. " Is it true that rapists frequently have a normal sexual outlet, either being married or having a steady girl friend?"

A. "Yes. A variety of studies have demonstrated that approximately fifty to sixty percent of rapists have been married at some time in their life, and the majority of rapists have had some other kind of sexual experience prior to engaging in a rape behavior."

Q. "Is there anything in the literature that tends to indicate that rapists have an abnormal sexual response, an unusual way of relating to the opposite sex?"

A. "Yes, there have been a variety of studies that have. One in particular, done in 1977, demonstrated that rapists experience sexual arousal to consenting as well as non-consenting or rape situations, on audio tapes. The control group listening to the same tapes experienced arousal to non-rape or consenting situations, but did not get aroused to the rape situations.

"Another finding of that study, which since has been replicated, was that rapists tend to misreport their degree of sexual arousal, whereas non-rapists tend to be much more accurate in their reporting of sexual arousal. This is consistent with the general notion that the rapists tend to distort their own experience in terms of the activities that they engage in."

Q. "There was voyeurism in this situation. Is that common?"

A. "In a lot of rape situations in which there are multiple offenders, the dynamics operating amount to a facilitation effect; that is, of one person encouraging the other, and some kind of diffusion of responsibility at the same time. The thinking is, 'Joe is doing it, then I can do it. If he is engaging in it, it's probably not so bad.'

"Another dynamic often present is that of gaining some esteem in the eyes of other people involved in the activity. A gang rapist may feel he is proving his masculinity."

WILL HE RAPE AGAIN?

Rapists who are caught often have a history of assault or sex offenses. But each time someone commits a crime, he may increase his chances of being caught.

His future behavior is not your responsibility, however. It is not up to you to stop him. If you can report to the police and participate in the legal process in an attempt to bring him into the system, that's courageous. But if you can't, whatever crimes he commits after that are not "because" you didn't report, but because he is still doing it.

If you know the rapist and confront him and he promises he will change, do not accept that statement unless he has done something to make it happen. Denial, addiction, desire for power, alcohol—all make sex offenders difficult to change. A mere promise is never enough.

FOR FAMILY AND FRIENDS

Even a family member who initially believed your charge and promised to get the offender help may back down as the shock wears off. It is easier for a family member to find a different explanation of what happened, or believe that the victim was at fault, than to believe a son, husband or brother is a rapist.

WHAT HAPPENS TO HIM IF HE IS CAUGHT? WILL HE COME BACK?

You may find that what happens to the rapist if he is caught and found guilty of the assault does not match your idea of justice or what should happen. You may hope he gets treatment, only to find that he is going to jail. You may hope he goes to jail so he can't hurt others or as punishment for what he did, only to find that he is required to attend counseling, and be on probation. This may feel as if nothing has happened to him.

You may be frightened to go outside, feel like a prisoner in your own house, while he seems to be getting off scot free. That may be an accurate perception, or he may be undergoing considerable changes.

Possibly the worst of all outcomes is that a jury or judge does not believe the evidence against him, and finds him not guilty. In that situation, at least he was forced to face legal proceedings. Sometimes that is a serious consequence.

This uncertainty of outcome can be disillusioning. Our society is still not sure how to view the common rapist. It seems obvious that the crazy stranger is terrible and should be locked up, but less certainty exists about how the twenty year old is to be treated, or the upperclass executive, or the man who rapes his secretary.

A few horrifying cases of rapists returning after prison have happened. Women who do not report also risk the return of the rapist. The greatest majority of cases involve neither. For you, though, that may not be enough comfort.

You can try to have the system inform you if the rapist is released on bail or from prison. The most difficult thing to accept is that there is not perfect security and the system doesn't work very well to protect victims/witnesses.

FOR FAMILY AND FRIENDS

You may want to spend some of your frustration and anger on judicial, treatment or prison reform. True prevention will find a way to treat offenders so they don't attempt to rape any more, identify young offenders early, find techniques to identify high risk offenders, and take the damage and destruction to humans seriously enough to develop the resources to restrain those at high risk of raping again.

DOES EVERYONE WHO IS ABUSED BECOME AN ABUSER?

No. As more is learned about how often boys are assaulted, it will become clear that although some boys become men who act out aggressively, committing sexual violence, others do not. Girls who are sexually abused become sexually aggressive much less frequently, although it does happen.

If you are concerned about your own capability for violence because you are experiencing intense rage and anger, know that the rage and anger are normal. If you find yourself drinking heavily or rationalizing any behavior, find professional help for yourself.

FOR FAMILY AND FRIENDS

Professional help for sexual aggression must be specialized. Most therapists are not experienced with the issues, the anger, the rage, and the need for confrontation and behavior change. Too many professionals are like everyone else, more comfortable minimizing the capacity of others for violence.

CAN I TRUST ANYONE?

All this information about rapists doesn't necessarily answer your questions about how anyone could do such a thing to someone else, or help you decide who to trust.

People are trustworthy to varying degrees and in different ways. Someone who can't be trusted to show up on time might be trusted never to be violent. What makes a person trustworthy?

Signs that someone is trustworthy might be:

- Someone listens to you and doesn't ignore or try to explain away your feelings.
- His actions match what he says he will do.
- He is willing to understand you and not make fun of you.
- He treats you respectfully. You are comfortable around him.

FOR FAMILY AND FRIENDS

You may feel as if you are having to prove yourself. Understand that it is an act of courage for her to trust you at all, to risk her safety with any man right now. Even old, close friends may seem dangerous to her.

I STILL DON'T UNDERSTAND

You may never understand the rapist or feel justice was done. At some point you need to stop trying to understand and go on with your own life, and turn your focus to yourself.

- You can't fix the rapist.
- His behavior is not your responsiblity.
- Think of men who have treated you well, who have not taken advantage of your trust.
- You are a survivor.
- You may need time to mourn your losses. If the rapist was someone very close to you, a husband, a man you had been dating for a long time, or someone you had hoped for a closer relationship with, you suffered the loss of that relationship and the life you had seen with him. You can even still care about him, and still need to go on.

FOR FAMILY AND FRIENDS

After you have learned what you need to know about the rapist(s), remember that your loved one needs to be your focus. She needs your energy for her, not focused on the rapist.

10

Making Choices About Safety

I'm worried about self protection now. If I had known how badly hurt I would be, I might have made different choices. How do I decide whom to trust? I thought I could trust my feelings. I don't know how to decide. How can I be safer? I don't want to give in to the fear. I don't want to live my life in a cage. Are there no easy answers?

I'M WORRIED ABOUT SELF PROTECTION NOW

Taking greater precautions after an assault does make sense. Some studies show that someone who has been assaulted once is more likely to be assaulted again. This is a trend, not an inevitability.

Many factors may increase someone's vulnerability. After an assault, energy is tied up in the recovery process. Deciding who to trust and who not to is harder.

A change in living circumstances may make you more vulnerable. Times of change are times of vulnerablity. Your energy is spent just finding your way around, learning the neighborhood patterns, and isn't available for general awareness.

You may feel more fragile and less ready to be rude to someone new who invades your space.

Making changes slowly and with an awareness of the risks can help protect you.

Ask others for help in making the adjustment. And learn to use tools for protection as you feel ready.

FOR FAMILY AND FRIENDS

You walk a fine line between helping protect her, and limiting her freedom because of the danger of rape. Recognize that your need for her to be safe may conflict with her need to go on with her life. You can offer your ideas about risk, and suggestions about minimizing it, but she should have the freedom to make the final decision.

IF I HAD KNOWN HOW BADLY HURT I WOULD BE, I MIGHT HAVE MADE DIFFERENT CHOICES.

In evaluating risk, the extent of damage done by rape is rarely understood.

Without an understanding of the damage rape causes, it is easy to ignore risks. The sense that it "won't happen to me," also keeps people from taking precautions.

You are now deciding about risks with the knowledge of the damage you have lived through, and the knowledge that it can happen to you.

As you get better you will want to move around more freely, return to work, school, or other activities. Then you must make choices about risks you are willing to take.

You can increase your safety by being much more conscious of the choices you are making. You may have relied on your feelings to tell you about danger. If you suffer from fear responses, you need to override your feelings and do some things anyway. But if you take that override too far, you will ignore signals of risk. You need to rely much more on thinking about the situation.

FOR FAMILY AND FRIENDS

If you are helping her make choices about risk, remember that the greatest publicity is about stranger rape, but the greatest number of assaults are by acquaintances.

HOW DO I DECIDE WHOM TO TRUST?

"For a woman to survive unraped, particularly in an urban setting, she must learn basic mistrust."
–Pauline Bart

Some people would suggest that you trust no one. But it is difficult to live that way, and you don't learn to discriminate between possibly trustworthy people and dangerous people by not trusting anyone.

Psychological self-defense, assertiveness, rudeness, and awareness are partners in self-protection. Being willing to stand up for what you want and don't want with strangers and with those close to you is the first step of deciding who to trust. You can't simply look at people and decide if they are safe. Or decide that because you know them or they are in your circle of friends, they are trustworthy. It is through interaction that you can gain some sense of how much they are willing to respect your wishes, even if the wishes aren't totally rational.

Rudeness is sometimes necessary to protect yourself. Some people don't care what you want or need and the only protection from them is to be rude, to yell at them or be willing to hurt their feelings. Someone who says, "What's the matter, don't you trust me?" deserves a flat "No."

FOR FAMILY AND FRIENDS

You can encourage her ability to stand up for herself. Only practice provides the skill. If it is never practiced, using it in a situation of extreme stress and fear is very unlikely.

I THOUGHT I COULD TRUST MY FEELINGS

Deciding who to trust after an acquaintance rape means deciding whether or not you missed cues, or if the rapist was too willing to lie and act for anyone to have avoided him.

If you decide you didn't miss any cues, you may not choose to do anything differently. But there are two factors which need consideration if you are to take care of yourself. One is to realize that the sexual assault may have influenced your belief about how well you deserve to be treated. One of the effects of rape is lowered self-esteem. You may feel less like you deserve good treatment, and less willing to assert your opinions or needs.

A need for excitement or intensity can also increase your risk. Sometimes life without crisis seems boring after a high level of fear or anxiety. Sometimes it is tempting to look for excitement to break the unbearable deadness or tediousness of day to day recovery. This can lead to additional risks. No one wants the abuse which may go with the risks. They don't know how to find other kinds of excitement.

Taking risks can lower your anxiety level too. If you have the sense of a hovering disaster, plunging into danger can actually take that low level anxiety away, and give you excitement instead of dread. That can reinforce, or make it more likely that you will take risks again. It is safer for you to face and live through the dread.

FOR FAMILY AND FRIENDS

Family members watching this risk-taking behavior can find it agonizing. Intervention can sound judgemental and blaming. Understanding that you cannot protect her, that she must learn her own self-protection tools, is the only comfort there is.

I DON'T KNOW HOW TO DECIDE

Much safety information is directed toward preventing stranger rape. Some measures require financial resources. For instance, having a car in good running order is safer than having one which breaks down. Public transportation may expose you to more risk from strangers. You may need to take those risks, but you can minimize your sense of jeopardy.

Research about rape isn't as helpful as it might be in helping assess self-protection measures. The presence of people makes rape less likely. But that doesn't mean you must give up walks in the woods. If you rarely encounter people there, the odds of a person being a rapist are very low, although not zero.

Some environments that have a reputation for being risky may not be avoidable. If you work late or irregular shifts, you may need to acknowledge a particular level of risk and take precautions. Knowing rapists often plan attacks suggests that areas of high use by potential victims are areas of risk. College campuses, jogging trails, and bars may be in this category. But it doesn't mean the answer is to avoid them totally. It means being aware of the potential danger as you would if you climbed mountains.

FOR FAMILY AND FRIENDS

Help her learn to respond to danger appropriately. Don't ask her to avoid all danger. It is too limiting.

HOW CAN I BE SAFER?

Rape victims are of all ages, but the ages between fourteen and twenty-nine seem to be those of greatest risk. Whether this reflects the greater mobility and higher exposure of younger women, or the fact that offenders tend to be younger, or that reporting patterns are different, hasn't been settled by studies. This does not mean that anyone at any age is totally safe.

Stable relationships may lessen your risk. One study of teenagers found that the one factor most clearly linked to sexual assault was the number of family crises in the prior year. Other studies have indicated that times of upheaval and change are also times of greater vulnerablity. Divorce, moving, loss of a partner through death; all throw people into new situations without their usual resources. These are times to be more on guard, less assuming.

Mourning, grieving and recovering, rather than denying, should help you be safer by allowing all of your energies to go into living today. Denial can create curious blind spots in your perceptions of others. Sometimes it seems as if what is most denied is most likely to happen again. Denial can create repetitive cycles of greater risk.

FOR FAMILY AND FRIENDS

Learn what you can about rape and the factors which lead to it, but don't scare her with the information.

I DON'T WANT TO GIVE INTO THE FEAR

Many rape victims feel better after they have learned some form of physical self-defense, karate, etc. The physical exercise and sense of power these tools provide are very healing. Some women who know these tools have been able to respond with anger to street approaches and protect themselves. They can be useful outlets too for learning to channel anger into protective energy and to defuse it safely.

One study found that concern about being raped was associated with avoiding rape, while concern about being killed or mutilated was associated with non-avoidance. The study also found that if flight from the situation was not possible then, trying one method of fighting back and then another was the most successful strategy. Learning self-defense gives you more power to make those choices and skills to think them through.

FOR FAMILY AND FRIENDS

Encourage her to learn physical self-defense if she shows an interest. Be careful of your own competitive responses to her new strength. Don't ask her to test what she is learning with you.

I DON'T WANT TO LIVE MY LIFE IN A CAGE

None of this should be taken to say that rape is the victim's responsibility. These measures are called self-protection, not prevention, because prevention happens when assailants are no longer creating harm. Acknowledging risk does not mean assuming blame.

When people drive on a weekend night between the hours of 11:00 and 2:00 their risk of being hit by a drunk driver is higher. That does not make it their fault if an accident happens. The cost of avoiding all risk in life is too high. Self protection means taking whatever measures make you feel safe and taking the risks you either must take to continue living, or those you feel willing to take.

Jogging is another example. Some advice to women runners says they should not run alone. But if you don't run alone, you might not run. Maybe you love to run. So you take the risks involved, and at the same time you attempt to protect yourself by noticing cars and people you have seen before. You could add a dog as a running partner. A dog can help you feel safer even if it is not protective. If a woman is raped when running, there are those who will say, "What did she expect?" and others who will say, "Anybody should have the right to run without risk of being assaulted." It is a risk each woman must decide about.

FOR FAMILY AND FRIENDS

Remember there is no way to keep someone totally safe.

ARE THERE NO EASY ANSWERS?

There are no easy answers on the question of safety.

It is always difficult to talk about self-protection without sounding like there was something any individual rape victim could have done. Everyone does the best they can or they would do differently. Although you may feel now you made a mistake in judgement, you probably made that same decision other times without someone lying in wait to hurt you.

Many rapes are a combination of factors coming together. You've always run the same route, but never saw that car before. You've seen that neighbor many times, but he has never come to the door when your husband wasn't home. You babysat for that couple many times but the man had never taken you home when he had been drinking before. It may be easy to look back and see what you could have done differently, but you had no way to predict the future. Now, with new knowledge and new fears, you may choose to make different decisions. Some of those may not be based on "realistic" fears. It is up to you. But making new choices does not mean you were at fault with your old choices.

FOR FAMILY AND FRIENDS

Now that you understand the circumstances which led up to the rape and see the ways it might have been avoided, it can become difficult to avoid believing the victim contributed. The responsiblity for the assault must continue to rest on the rapist.

11

I Laughed Today

I can't believe it, but for days I haven't thought about being raped. I joked with my kids. I won't ever forget what happened. The world looks different to me. I'm more careful about trusting. I don't even take "victim blaming" personally anymore. I'm getting better. I don't need to be a saint.

I CAN'T BELIEVE IT, BUT FOR DAYS I HAVEN'T THOUGHT ABOUT BEING RAPED

Recovery means no longer feeling totally defined and controlled by the experience of being victimized. One of the ways this is reflected is by thinking of yourself as a survivor, not just of the attack, but of the effects of the rape. One does not become a survivor quickly. To deny the damage of the victimization can be an attempt to shortcut some of the emotional, psychological steps in healing. To attempt to define yourself as recovered too quickly can create a tremendous burden for you to carry.

To return to your previous level of functioning could certainly be recovery, and it sounds easy. But it isn't, and it suggests that you can go back to your life as it was before it was interrupted. Recovery means more than survival, more than a simple patching back together again.

FOR FAMILY AND FRIENDS

Your recovery and her recovery will move at different speeds and in different directions. It is okay to laugh, find beauty in things, enjoy life, as you find yourself ready to.

Your recovery can be marked in part by your ability to see her as a competent capable person, and not a victim.

I JOKED WITH MY KIDS

Recovery is laughter at a joke,
crying at a movie,
enjoying a friend,
finding joy in sun, rain, snow, everyday events,
    flowers, art or children,
feeling again.

Recovery is more than an absence of symptoms, although you would probably settle for that. Some of the effects may never leave you, but you recover nonetheless. One of the signs you've recovered is that you can feel the little things in life, enjoy them, be saddened by them, and not get stuck in them.

At first you may be startled by forgetting, and not trust the everyday feelings as real. You may be guarded and careful waiting to get hit again by the old awful feelings.

Eventually you give yourself and others permission to laugh and forget for a while. Recovery is being able to sleep, eat and enjoy sexual pleasure.

FOR FAMILY AND FRIENDS

At first feelings are too frightening and overwhelming and even good ones are damped out. Recovery is being less frightened of feelings and experiencing ups and downs as just part of life.

I WON'T EVER FORGET WHAT HAPPENED

Recovery is knowing that some pieces of you are changed in ways you wouldn't have chosen, and living with that.

It doesn't mean forgetting.

Recovery means more than going back to who you were before, because that person has been irrevocably changed. You may have difficulty accepting the new person you have become: you may not like her as well. Recovery means going beyond that. Neither you nor your family can recreate the time before the rape.

Recovery means you mourn the life you might have had, choices you might have made, and person you might have been. It doesn't mean you can't retrieve many of those pieces, but some have been stolen from you forever. After all the intensity of feelings—fear, dread, anger—your sadness may feel insignificant. But it isn't.

FOR FAMILY AND FRIENDS

Rituals for mourning are difficult to create in this culture which so values happiness and a quick fix. You need to mourn, and give her permission to be sad too. Rituals can help give you both a way to do that.

THE WORLD LOOKS DIFFERENT TO ME

Recovery means you have found a way to hold loosely expectations of justice, revenge or recompense.

This means you can fight with intensity to change what you believe is wrong and have the balance to move on if you can't achieve what you had hoped. Recovery is finding a way to make an opportunity for a new beginning out of the unfairness, injustice, and violence. No one gets to chose their own barriers, handicaps, nightmares, or burdens.

Recovery is a balancing act between acceptance of how much of life can't be controlled and individual responsiblity as reflected in the Serenity Prayer, "Give me the serenity to accept what I cannot change, the strength to change what I can, and the wisdom to know the difference."

Those who struggle through the nightmare to the other side have wisdom about the world and how people behave. They have no illusions that all is within their control, nor are they out of control. They have encountered evil, terror, and death, and survived, more than survived, turned it to their use.

There is no justification for the time, energy and year(s) lost. But there is no choice to accepting losses. Railing against them is fine, but it changes nothing.

FOR FAMILY AND FRIENDS

You are equal in this need to understand what cannot be changed or controlled and what must be changed.

I'M MORE CAREFUL ABOUT TRUSTING

Recovery means having a revised sense of who is trustworthy and your own ability to assess that. Your initial reaction may be to decide not to trust anyone, or that you can't decide who to trust, so why even try.

But to live, you make decisions every day about who you can trust in some matters. Every time you drive, buy something, make a political decision, or believe something you read, you are making judgements about trust.

Recovery means understanding how difficult it is to know another, and not giving up, not becoming totally cynical and bitter.

FOR FAMILY AND FRIENDS

If you are helping her assess a situation, ask questions. It is too easy to impose on her your own version of how you see someone or a situation, especially while she is uncertain.

Once awareness of the risk of rape exists, this assessment of people goes on regardless of recovery. You and she simply gain confidence again in your judgements.

I DON'T EVEN TAKE "VICTIM BLAMING" PERSONALLY ANYMORE

Why look at victim blaming in recovery? Because you will continue to hear people blame victims. When efforts are made to relieve social problems—in this case, stop rapists—and those efforts fail, victim blaming becomes more intense. The more people try, and fail, to help, the more they need someone to blame.

Recovery is allowing yourself passionate disagreement with those who say "You can't make anyone do anything," and not becoming totally frustrated with the other's lack of understanding.

Recovery is knowing that others don't know and letting that be all right. You know that people who are victimized make people face realities they would rather avoid. You can decide when to use your own experience to educate others, and when to "let it slide."

Recovery is hearing platitudes and cliches without being compelled to act, no longer taking them personally.

FOR FAMILY AND FRIENDS

You will be free to decide when you want to spend the energy to change someone's mind about how and when rape occurs and who is responsible.

I'M GETTING BETTER

Recovery is thoughts of the future and how it is going to be, and believing that you will get there.

Recovery is smelling fear and not having to leave the store.

Recovery is hearing an engine roar and pop, and not surrendering to terror.

Recovery is being startled and not errupting in anger at the startler. It means being afraid and doing something anyway. It means fewer and fewer flashbacks. It means knowing that anniversaries are hard times, and that the pain passes.

Recovery means knowing that the sense of dread and anxiety doesn't reflect reality. It means understanding what you do to stop the feeling of anxiety, and having that behavior under your control most of the time.

FOR FAMILY AND FRIENDS

Your own sense of dread may be triggered by a time of year, a series of events, or a song you hear on the radio. You can mention that to her and see if she is feeling it too. Exploring together what triggers the feelings can help you both be more aware and creative in responding.

I DON'T NEED TO BE A SAINT

Recovery is successive acts of courage. But it doesn't mean being a saint. Getting healthy sometimes looks impossible. And being "totally" healthy is. Everyone carries around problems, which they handle more or less well depending on the circumstances of their life at any particular time.

Recovery most of all means that you know you can decide how you are and have the tools and knowledge to continue.

It also means you know you will recycle your experiences many times. One of the ways you may do that is to work with others who are victimized, when you are ready.

FOR FAMILY AND FRIENDS

Recovery means you no longer see a dividing line, but have a clear sense of equality with her in trying to make sense out of a world of events without apparent meaning.

12

Notes For Therapists

Given the statistics that one in three women are victims of sexual violence sometime in their lives, most therapists will eventually work with clients who are recovering from a rape. Some of the issues are not any different from those you face everyday. But the crisis created by rape causes uncertainty. Rape attacks all aspects of a human being—the physical, emotional, psychological and spiritual. It is a brush with death that shatters all defenses. Because of societal misunderstandings it can jeopardize relationships, work, and even housing.

This chapter gives some guidelines about issues particular to rape victims and attempted rape victims, who may have some or all of the same symptoms. This short section cannot make you an expert in all the areas you would eventually want to know about if you were to specialize in treating sexual assault victims. Nearly all forms of therapy are of some use to someone victimized by sexual violence. It is useful to know about post traumatic stress disorders, sexuality, family dynamics, alcohol abuse, eating disorders, racism, and homophobia in addition to understanding the dynamics of rape and recovery.

No matter what your expertise your primary task is to provide a safe and respectful place for the rape victim to assess where she is in recovery and choose her next steps. Your client will be in one of three stages of recovery. She may be in crisis, she may be muddling through, or she may need help with the final process of integration.

Someone in crisis might come to you because she previously saw you for a time and completed a round of therapy. Now she returns for help because she has been raped. Or a current client may have recently been raped, in the last week, between appointments. The victim in crisis is unlikely to be a new client, unless her family brings her.

You may see someone who was victimized a short time ago, but she does not name the rape as the reason she is coming to you. However, resolving the losses and issues created by a rape may be critical to resolution of the problems she comes in for. She may not be able to name specific complaints, only that things aren't going right, that she feels awful and doesn't know why. She may not associate her symptoms with a rape. The victimization will only surface as you ask about circumstances around the time she started feeling badly. Asking about sexual assault has become part of many therapists' intake process.

Someone at this "muddling through" stage might also come to you asking for specific help with relationships, sexual difficulties, fear, eating problems, or just so that she can speed up the recovery process by getting help. She might come to therapy because she is frightened by flashbacks or violent dreams and doubts her own sanity.

You may see someone who has moved a long way through the recovery process but needs some help with the final difficult stages of moving through the anger, finding appropriate ways to let go of what happened, and grieving.

You may also have a client who was raped in the past, yet doesn't see it as having any relationship to current issues. Part of your assessment is to be sure she has made that determination based on an understanding of the recovery process.

Although it is difficult to put time spans on stages that are not totally discrete, some guidelines suggest that the crisis stage lasts from a few days to a month, the next stage of coping in a variety of ways lasts from a few months to many years, and the integration stage often doesn't start before six months have passed, and can take years depending on the nature of the assault. People move through stages at very different rates. Residual effects, specifically fear, have been documented for as long as three years.

The length of time since the rape, and the level of difficulty she is encountering will to a large extent determine your approach. Each of the three stages requires a somewhat different approach.

You may wonder whether it is better for a female sexual assault victim to work with a man or a woman. The assumption is often made that victims would rather talk with a woman. And some would. If you are working with someone and she reveals she has been victimized, she trusts you enough to begin work with you. Whether you are a man or a women may not be very important.

Initial Crisis

The most likely person to walk into your office, throw herself into a chair and say something happened last weekend, she thinks she was raped, is an adolescent you have been working with. Studies such as Diana Russell's in San Francisco have suggested the most vulnerable ages are from fifteen to twenty-five.

This suggests several issues that are important immediately. First, you may not understand why she doesn't know whether what happened was rape. Often adolescent women understand and can name stranger rape as rape but are very puzzled about what to call it when an acquaintance uses force. Help her understand that any time force or the the threat of force is used to obtain sexual contact, it is rape. Whether or not it can be legally prosecuted is another issue. Laws differ from state to state about levels of force and resistance and how the law views previous relationships between the victim and the offender. Date rape, marital rape, rape by the boss, are not prosecuted in many jurisdictions. The age and race of the victim and the offender also may affect legal action. Your role is not to investigate the circumstances, but to take seriously what she has been through, even if she minimizes it at first.

Secondly, your belief about her responsibility for the assault will be tested. If she has been troubled, acting out, or involved in risky behavior, it may be tempting to treat this as just one more consequence of that risk-taking behavior. Although she may have taken some risks you consider unacceptable, what happened to her is far more cruel then anything she thought she would encounter. What she needs is your help dealing with very concrete issues about how to sleep, what to tell her parents, boyfriend, and teachers.

Victims in this early stage are very vulnerable to any statement that can be construed as blaming. Their normal defenses are weakened. The first question to ask is, "How are you doing?" not "What happened?" If she says that she is fine you can ask, "What decisions have you made so far?" This gives you an idea what she has considered, and probably what her areas of greatest concern are. She may be worried about how other people will react. She may be worried about pregnancy, losing her boyfriend, or losing her independence—being restricted or told to return from college or a distant city by her parents. (Elderly victims also experience this fear of loss of independence. They fear this may be the justification their adult children use to push them to move.)

Take time to center yourself and move slowly. It's very difficult to stay non-judgemental and avoid taking control when confronted with this crisis. And even though you may want to know how this person could have been raped, what the circumstances were, and so on, this is usually not the time to ask those questions. You also may have a very clear sense of what she should do—get medical care, report to the police, and confide in those around her to get support—but she may not be ready to do any of those things.

If she is a new client, this is also not the time to gather historical or background information, except as it applies to her resources for coping with this crisis.

You will be most helpful if she sees she can trust you to respect her limits and help her with the issues *she* considers important. You can ask what her thoughts are about medical care or reporting to the police, and provide accurate information if she lacks it. She may need to know how she can get confidential medical care or other help. If she didn't report to the police you can ask how she made that decision. You need to be careful of "Why" questions because they sound like a request for her to justify her decision. "Why" is a word that suggests judgement or blaming and opens distance between you. You just want to know if she made the decision based on sound information or if she believes something she saw on television that isn't accurate.

You will also want to sort your own information very carefully. A new law may have been passed that increases victim protection or rights in some way, but may not apply yet, or in the particular jurisdiction where your client was victimized. Before you offer any reassuring information you need to check with the local rape crisis center, police, or legal department. Treatment of victims has improved in the past fifteen years, but some parts of the system are very resistant to change because they are charged with the constitutional protection of the accused.

You should be aware of your own need to believe that justice can be provided through the criminal justice system. If you work with this client for very long, you may have to help her deal with disillusionment about the criminal justice system. In this immediate crisis stage, your belief that justice can be provided through police reporting can get in the way of your hearing her needs.

You will want to ask how she is sleeping. Is she terrified at night? It's not unusual to be frightened at home even if the rape did not occur there. Again, explore what her resources are for safety measures. See Chapter One for suggestions.

Ask if she has returned to work or school. How is she doing there? Let her know that having trouble concentrating is not unusual and that it will get better, but probably slowly. She may feel boxed in by commitments she feels incapable of fulfilling. To the extent you can, help her understand that recovery from rape is more difficult than recovering from a severe auto accident or a serious illness. She may want to consider how she would take care of herself under those circumstances and use some of those same measures.

The other urgent issue for many victims is who to tell and what to tell. Many victims are afraid of the reactions of their families, boyfriends, husbands, and friends. They are afraid of hurting other people, of being blamed, of being labeled and of the many feelings generated by rape. They are afraid of the anger of others, the potential violence, the rejection. Sometimes these fears are based on a realistic perception of others, sometimes they aren't. You can approach this by asking what she would say *if* she told someone. After leaving your office she may find that the pressure to tell someone is much stronger than she expected. She is more likely to get support and feel good about telling if she has done some rehearsal.

If she is open to it and there is time, walk her through a realistic assessment of the reaction she fears from others and how she could respond. If she responds that her parents or husband will be mad, ask if that is their usual response. If she says yes, ask what they do when they are mad. She needs the support of important people in her life if it is possible to gain it. Most adolescents are certain their parents would be mad because of the circumstances of the rape. But often parents are supportive. Obviously, if she indicates any history of violence in her relationship, her assessment of the need for secrecy may be totally accurate.

If she decides that she wants to tell the significant people in her life, work with her on the words, the timing, and handling the reactions. She can say, "I was raped. I need your help. This is what I've done so far. Please don't be mad at me." Often people want to know what happened to try to make sense of the assault. Help your client decide how much she is willing to say, and when she wants to say, "That's too hard to talk about right now." The only time she needs to tell all the details is in a police report. Other than that she can determine what she says and when she wants to stop talking about it. A prepared response to the question "Why didn't you...?" can help her feel less helpless in the face of people's reactions.

You can't get too far in an initial hour with someone. Unless you have the option of extending her time, you need to deal with the most emerging issues, and set up another appointment soon. Someone in crisis might need one the next day. A week is too long unless she has another source of support, in addition to family and friends. You might suggest she call a local rape crisis center for additional support, if there is one in your community. You also need to set out your own rules. Can she call you between appointment times? Be careful about modifying your usual rules about home phone calls or other limits. You still need to take care of yourself.

The crisis stage may be resolved within a week or two. It can be extended by other events such as legal proceedings or a confrontation with the rapist. The feelings of this stage can be evoked by smells, sounds, or other reminders of the assault for many months, but they will be resolved more easily and quickly.

Your stance during this stage is a structured "How can I help?" You use your knowledge of dynamics and information about rape to ask about areas that may be causing distress, while leaving the decisions about what is most important to the victim. You support her courage in telling you, her survival, and her resources for recovery. You can provide both a safe place for genuine emotions to be expressed and basic information about the effects of sexual violence. A safe place means you can hear what this experience means to her without making judgements, becoming anxious yourself, or telling her what she should have done. You can provide reassurance that her symptoms are normal responses to rape and will disappear with time. And you have the expertise to recognize when a normal response has gone on too long and become destructive or self-perpetuating. Help her understand that recovery will take time but that it will happen. Help her set up a course for the future.

People in crisis lose cards, lose phone numbers, and forget appointment times. Expect to repeat yourself and check agreements. When you see her again, ask about any followup she was going to do and offer the numbers or information again.

After the intensity of the crisis stage has subsided, there may be some denial of how damaging the assault was. You may find that your client backs away from you and sees you as a reminder of the rape and the pain of those early days. You may need to spend some sessions in which not much seems to be happening. You can focus on the positive steps she has taken, although you want to be cautious about setting her up to be too strong. You don't want to participate in the natural tendency to minimize the damage she has suffered and you don't want to predict or define what is going to happen for her. This is a very difficult balance: she simultaneously needs your recognition of her strength and of the difficulty of her tasks.

If she reported to the police, you also may find yourself dealing with some of the fallout from the legal system. Each police report or procedure reopens wounds and recreates some of the early crisis. If the legal system doesn't take action, that may also create further disillusionment and despair. Your role is to help her separate her knowledge of what happened from the actions of those in the legal system. She may need help understanding that the inaction of the legal system is not based on the truth of what happened to her, but on a whole set of factors outside her control. See Chapter Three for some of the problems she may face. If you cannot be her advocate in the legal system be sure she finds someone to do that for her.

One technique you should avoid is telling stories about someone you know who has gone through a similar experience. Sometimes in an effort to make a victim comfortable, or to indicate knowledge of her situation, you might think about doing this. There are two problems with it. One is that she may worry that you will tell her story to someone else. She may also identify with the person you are describing to such an extent that she takes on more pain. Sexual violence creates very vivid pictures that are hard to shake. She doesn't need any more from you. Many victims find going to a group with other survivors very helpful. Seeing other women who have been through rape helps her realize that she is not alone, that there are other people who really do understand. Stories don't necessarily have that effect.

Muddling Through

After the initial crisis stage there is often a muddling through time. Victims attempt to return to their life as it was before the rape. The initial decisions about medical and legal care have been made and whatever is happening on those fronts is happening. People who must be told have been told.

If you have been seeing someone from the crisis stage, you may find later sessions spent on school or job difficulties, marriage problems, or problems with friends. You want to give her continued permission to talk about the rape and still have problems because of it, without seeming to pry or insist that she talk about it when she doesn't want to. You will continue to judge when to push just a little bit to confront problems you think are there because of the assault, and when to respect her limits and coping tools. In general it is best to err toward being respectful. Sometimes it works to simply say, "Sometimes people know others want them to be better, and want to be better so much themselves, that it makes it really hard to admit that there are still problems."

How much difficulty she has at this stage depends in part on the type of assault she suffered. There are some indications that victims of sudden stranger rapes that occur away from home have fewer long term difficulties. Difficulties increase markedly if there were multiple rapists, if the rapist was a trusted person, or if the rape occurred in the victim's home.

Fear is the most frequent residual symptom. Depression is also likely. Someone may come to you saying she just can't seem to get any better. She also may want your help assessing her own coping mechanisms. She may be concerned that she is drinking more than she should or because she has to go through long, compulsive routines to feel safe.

Again, you want to ask what decisions she made, how she came to those decisions, and ask if she is comfortable with those decisions at this stage. She may have some concrete problems she needs help with. She may wish she had made a police report and feel guilty about every rape she hears about. Or the criminal justice system may have failed her, not caught the rapist, not pressed charges, not convicted him, not sent him to prison, not done what she had hoped. She may need medical care to feel secure about her health, but fear getting it. She may not have told important people in her life and need to. Remember your own sense of what people should do may not be right for her. You may even want to express how difficult it is to make decisions during a crisis. Ask her "What did you know or think about that led you to that choice?"

She may be suffering severe disillusionment about herself and life, have lost all sense of meaning, but not understand the extent to which these feelings originate from the rape. Your role is to remember and understand her need to separate her disillusionment from the victimization. Denial and minimization are primary coping tools for some time in the recovery process. Admitting how badly she was hurt and how powerless she was to prevent the assault would force her into a painful examination of her shattered assumptions about the world. This makes it very difficult for her to connect the problems she is having to the victimization.

Discuss with her what creates the need for therapy now. Ask if she experiences phobias, flashbacks, depression. She may be afraid to mention these without a prompt, for fear that they mean she is crazy.

If she says she suddenly finds herself back in the assault, shaken and frightened and without any control over her thoughts, it may be reassuring to her to know those are called flashbacks and are considered a normal reaction to severe trauma. She is not going crazy. Then you can find out how often they occur, and if they are dangerous to her. Does she fear a flashback while driving a car or operating dangerous equipment? How can she increase her safety? The flashbacks will diminish with time and as other cathartic work is accomplished.

You can help her assess how limiting her fears are. Do they limit her functioning in ways that are unacceptable to her? For example many women live with the fear of being out alone at night and simply don't do it and don't feel excessively limited by it. But few would accept being unable to go out in daylight to go grocery shopping. Explore practical ways to continue living even with the increased fear level. A friend's company, changing patterns, or asking for shift changes may help.

If her fear creates panic, or if she has developed phobias, she needs your help and support getting appropriate treatment. Talking about the rape and her feelings about it may not be enough to change the developed fear patterns. Systematic desensitization or other specialized techniques may be more useful. If you are unable to provide the specialized treatment needed, your role will be to help her manage seeing the right specialist.

Other isssues may bring her to therapy. You may be seeing this person about difficulties in relationships and then you learn of the rape. Or eventually she may be open about difficulties with sexuality, ranging from lack of desire to addictive sexual behavior. She may be frightened by thoughts of suicide. Or she may be suffering from severely diminished self-esteem. She may be struggling with the reactions of others. They may have been supportive for a time, and then at some point expect a faster recovery. She may have come to you at their urging, but not be sure she needs to be there. Help her assess her needs at this point in the recovery process. You may want to spend some time asking about how she was doing before the assault to develop an accurate picture of her recovery needs. Emphasize how serious an injury to the self a rape is, that patience is needed, and that working on one problem at a time has the most possibility of success.

Set short term goals with her about what she hopes to accomplish in therapy. Clear goals can provide her some hope about getting better and some definition to the muddle of her life.

At some time during this work, after some trust has been established, it is useful to ask about the details of the rape and to work through what happened. She may be relieved that she has found someone who is not afraid to hear what happened to her. Stating your willingness to listen gives her the permission to talk about it. She may not have told anyone certain details of the assault. You may need to prompt her by saying that you know rape often involves forms of sexual contact people are sometimes ashamed of or embarrassed about.

Both talking about the rape and hearing about it are very painful. They can trigger earlier crisis feelings or flashbacks. Both you and the victim need to be prepared and ready to begin this process. You need to be sure to leave closure and re-entry time. You need to have a way to process and release the pain you take on. You need to take care of yourself.

To let go of some of the pain, she needs to sense your empathy and willingness to hear side by side with her, not judging or seeing her as different, not examining her. She probably protects other people close to her from the horror of the rape. She needs to be able to share it somehow. Telling about the rape can be a relief and help her begin to understand and release some of the pain created by it.

You may need to help some women find the words or way to express what happened. They may not know any language except slang for what happened. You can give permission for her to use the words she knows, or provide descriptions and words if she would find them helpful. Do not assume on the basis of age, race, or any other characteristic that someone is comfortable with slang for sexual behavior. It can be a jolt to a victim to hear what happened to her described in slang she would never use.

You don't want to do this before adequate trust has developed. You don't want to do it when she doesn't want to. You cannot do it if you are not in a position to hear the horror. And you don't want to avoid it because of your own denial about what happens to people. Your own feelings may need some work before you are prepared to do this. If you can't hear her without distancing yourself it may be better not to ask, and to work with those issues you are comfortable with. You also don't want to do this kind of intense work every session. She needs breaks from facing the pain, as do you.

Related Issues

This process of working through the experience is most useful in working directly on the effects of the rape. Other issues can interfere with doing that and need attention too.

Alcohol is a societally accepted method of numbing pain. If you believe someone's primary problem is alcohol abuse, attend to that first. If the alcohol use has been a coping method, it is possible to suggest replacement methods of dealing with the pain, developing some tolerance for it, and moving past the need for alcohol as you help her process the rape trauma.

Other problems to check on are loss of appetite, compulsive eating, and compulsive shopping. Be sure you find out whether these problems existed before the assault. If they have arisen as a situational response, they should be easier for her to replace with healthier behavior.

Sexual problems after a rape vary widely. At first she may believe she doesn't have any problems, trying to minimize the damage done to her and hoping she can make that so by experiencing a postive sexual relationship. She may experience problems after more time has passed and have a very difficult time mentioning them. You may want to ask, "How is your sexual relationship with your partner?" at reasonable intervals. Do not assume she is heterosexual when you ask these questions.

You may have an educational role to serve: talking about normal sexuality, problems people sometimes experience in response to rape, and working with her to make changes she needs to make. You may want to refer her to a women's health clinic for information about her body and reassurance about her health. If she is in a lesbian relationship and having difficulties, she may be reassured to learn that is not unusual.

You also may need to help someone cope with cultural beliefs that put a high value on virginity. Although you may disagree with that value, it is a real problem for many women who feel worthless because of the sexual contact. You may need to ask questions about her culture. How can she be forgiven? Are there people within her culture who understand that rape is beyond the victim's control? Are they working within the culture to change beliefs? What does her culture say she should do now that this has happened? Can she reach her anger at the injustice done to her by those beliefs? Is that anger useful or is there another way she can work to lessen the impact of those beliefs?

You may want to help her work on a definition of consent. Consent is not the same as submission. Consent is based on choice. It is active, not passive. Consent is possible only when there is equal power. Giving in because of fear is not consent.

As you identify and work on problems and resolve those most immediately related to the assault, sessions may drift more and more toward problems with school, work, or relationships. She may need your permission and help to continue talking and examining the effects of the violence. She may believe she should be better than she is. You can continue to provide reassurance that recovery takes time, and help her see the progress she has made. You may want to reassess and set some new goals with her. She may need you to suggest possible avenues to continue recovery: exploring anger, grieving the losses, forgiving herself, and developing new assumptions about safety and trust.

Integration

Besides dealing with symptoms generated directly by the rape, several other emotional issues may need resolution: anger without a legitimate target, violent dreams or thoughts, grief, new ways to feel safe, whom and when to trust, racial issues if any, and heightened feelings of vulnerability caused by disabilities.

Both victims and family members may find anger associated with the assault difficult to handle. The anger can't legally be directed in its full measure toward the rapist. Some people believe being angry is wrong, or shows they aren't nice people. Men and women tend to react differently in response to anger. Men may feel the manly thing to do is to beat up the rapist. Women may be frightened that anger will lead to further violence. Both men and women can be afraid that they are going to act out their anger and harm an innocent bystander or one of the people they care about.

Rape victims frequently have violent dreams. Soon after the rape they typically relive the assault in their dreams. Later they may dream of themselves acting out violence toward others. This can be very frightening too, but is a sign that she is healing. Sometimes taking back the power in the dream is a dramatic healing step. Certainly she needs to be reassured that those dreams do not mean she is more likely to commit a violent act.

Some people believe a victim isn't healing until she experiences her anger and acts it out in some cathartic way. For some survivors anger is a healing, powerful force leading them to feel energized and strong. Anger is an important and dramatic step toward placing the responsiblity on the rapist.

But studies about anger suggest that for others who highly value control, serenity, and composure, anger is frightening. It signals being out of control rather than taking back power. They may even feel robbed of their former selves by the anger they feel. Your role is to find out how your client has dealt with anger in the past, how she feels about that coping mechanism, and whether she wants to find a way to use that one again or build a new one.

You may also want to explore other emotions that have energized the client in the past. Grief, pain, and fear also can provide energy for action and healing.

If someone is consistently abused or overpowered because of a refusal to use anger to power self-protection, you may want to explore how she learned that anger was never useful. You may need to help her find a way to use it or another emotion in her own behalf. Look at other emotions that might energize her to take action. Love of children moves many women. Some women have a long history of learning that anger only results in retaliation. Using her anger may be part of how she learns to be safe again. Some who work to heal sexual violence see anger as allowing the transformation from victim to survivor to warrior. As you work with her you need to be very aware that self-protection work can trigger feelings of self-blame. She may think, "If only I had known this, taken this class, or understood who a rapist might be..." She may feel she should never have trusted anyone or that she shouldn't have taken a risk she did. She may feel guilty about her own inability to fight back.

Your role is to help her make choices about the risks she is willing to take that are not horribly limiting. It is not an acceptable option to live a life in a cage. And the decision to just take chances because the worst has already happened may be very dangerous.

You may want to suggest she take a self-defense class if you know of one that is careful of past victims. Classes conducted without that awareness can be hurtful and reinforce a sense of powerlessness by suggesting that there are right and wrong ways to respond to an attack. Some responses are more likely to be successful in avoiding a rape, but there are no guarantees. Mock attack situations can also create flashbacks for victims. Your client needs to be prepared to take care of herself.

Talking about safety, risks, and choices may lead to discussion of self-blame and self-forgiveness. Recovery requires that she find a way to put that self-blame to rest. In the early stages, self-blame may be useful protection from the knowledge that she had no control over what happened to her. Eventually she needs to believe that although she might not make the same choice again, she did the best she could at the time with the knowledge she had. And she is not a bad, terrible, or stupid person for making that choice. Help her come to that belief by asking her questions that help her see how she is judging herself based on information she didn't have at the time of the assault.

As she discovers her own method of making choices about risk, she will often want to sort out issues about men and the ability of some to rape. Being very cautious of all men, and trusting none, may work for some women. Intimate relationships with men may not be important to them. Be careful of assumptions that victims are heterosexual and want relationships with men.

For a client who does want relationships with men, you can explore her history of relationships. Does she know any men she considers kind and without potential for violence against women? Who are they and what are their characteristics? If she knows no men even as friends who seem trustworthy, you may want to explore how she forms friendships. Does she let others pick her without regard for her likes and dislikes? Help her form a picture of how a trustworthy man would act. Help her begin to decide what *she* wants in a relationship.

A major task of reconstructing a life after victimization is to examine and reconstruct the assumptions that allow functioning in the world. Without those assumptions life feels meaningless and chaotic. Some women may be able to rebuild spiritual faith. Others may need to find a new basis for faith. Victims find their beliefs about God severely challenged. This encounter with evil may bring a crisis in faith. You can't ignore this need, nor can you assume that she will be helped in her religious community. Explore with her carefully what she thinks the response of her religious leaders would be if she went to them for help with her questions of faith. If you know of community resources working in religious communities on issues of domestic and sexual violence, you might suggest she contact them.

You can help her remember what the sources of meaning were in her life before the assault. Can some of them be recaptured? Encourage her to try things even when she feels it won't be helpful. Repetition of old routines can be reassuring and restore some sense of meaning if enough time has passed.

As she moves through these steps help her understand how much she has recovered. Recovery is a very uneven process, and setbacks can be very discouraging. She also needn't be "perfectly" healthy before she and you decide she is as free of the shadows as she is going to be for a while.

She should leave therapy with:
- a strong sense that she is not alone.
- an understanding of the phenomenon of rape and sexual violence in our culture.
- a sense of control over her life.
- a sense of physical well-being and knowledge that she can take care of herself and her body.
- peace with her decision about reporting to the police and taking legal action.
- sexuality neither buried nor expressed indiscriminately or self- destructively.
- freedom from alcohol or drug dependence.
- increased self-esteem.
- freedom from the desire to get revenge on the offender.
- the ability to choose to tell or not tell her story.
- an ability to trust when she chooses to trust.

- freedom from guilt or self-blame.
- memories of the rape that no longer threaten to overwhelm her.
- progress from victim to survivor and maybe to warrior.
- a new picture of her world and her place in it.

When you and she agree she has closed the process for now, help her find ritual ways to demonstrate that closure and to celebrate. Acknowledge her courage.

Special Considerations

Men as Victims

We have spoken of victims as female. Men are raped too, as are adolescent boys. Males are much less likely to tell you, but if someone reveals he has been raped your initial responses should be similar. Ask what he has done and who has been told. Men tend to be much more secretive, less likely to report to the police, less able to ask for help, and more fearful of others' reactions.

Men suffer different damage to self-image. Powerlessness can be the key issue rather than fear. If he wasn't as tough or aggressive as he thought he should be, he suffers damage to his picture of himself as a man. Sometimes fear of being or becoming homosexual is raised because most rapists of men are men. Reactions to anger may also be different. He needs to know he is not alone. This has happened to other men. It doesn't happen just in prisons. And as with a female victim, proceed slowly and respectfully. You can learn what you need to as issues surface.

Assaults in the Distant Past

Frequently a therapist learns about an assault that happened in the distant past. Assessing the current effects of those assaults is difficult. Because of the role of denial and the difficulty of working through the last stages, it is wise to be cautious about accepting a statement that rape does not create current problems. Ask some respectful questions. Someone who shows clear sorrow about what happened, can describe changes she went through, and knows the price she paid probably has integrated the experience. You won't get a sense of brittleness or rigid control. Don't forget to support the hard work she had to do to reach the place where she is.

A flat, gritted-teeth voice is an indication of emotional weight on the experience. Again, you need to be respectful of her readiness to deal with the pain. You also need to be careful of assumptions that current difficulties cannot be resolved without resolving or working on the rape experience. You can ask, "Do you think it would be useful to explore your feelings about that experience? They could be related to your current problems." If she says "no," leave it alone. She's probably not ready to relive that pain. The timing of that should be up to her. If she does decide to work on it, the pain may be very fresh. She may experience some shock and crisis. You can reassure her that that is normal.

You may find as you work with a client who has been recently victimized that she tells you of an additional past experience. This does not reflect on her credibility. Repeated victimization may suggest chronic problems about choices, but not necessarily. She may need help with a secondary sense of injustice if she believed that she wouldn't be raped again. Some people make sense of an assault with a thought such as, "I've paid the price" or "Lightening doesn't strike twice in the same place." Reactions to both assaults may be mixed up.

Childhood sexual assault victims are also recognizing their need for help. Recovery from childhood abuse has different dynamics that you should be familar with to help someone work on those issues.

If you work with women recovering from the effects of abusive relationships, be aware that resolving issues about sexual assault may also be important. At least half of physically abusive relationships also involve sexual violence.

Significant Others

If her family is available to work with you, you may help her by spending some time with them. With limited time you may feel torn between spending time with the victim or her family. But if she has support from her family, her immediate recovery may be easier. Sometimes the easiest way for a victim to reveal to her significant others what has happened is in a session with a counselor. You will need to discuss with the victim what you can and can't reveal about the circumstances of the assault before you begin talking with family members.

Rape creates a crisis for the whole family. You can be helpful to the family by suggesting ways they can help the victim, and ways they can take care of themselves. You want to explain to them that she is very vulnerable to any statements that sound blaming. They may need help avoiding blaming the victim out of their own sense of helplessness and anger. Validating the sense of frustration about not being able to protect those they love can be useful. No one ever deserves to be raped, and no one ever expects it to happen to her no matter what risks she takes. But husbands, fathers, or mothers who have spent enormous energy trying to protect a wife or child with rules may have a hard time understanding that the victim is not to blame. The best you may be able to do is to ask that those reactions at least be postponed until the victim has recovered. Her family may require help understanding that the victim needs to make the decisions about police reporting, medical care, and who is told. You can also help family members understand that they have their own recovery process. They too have suffered a loss, a failure, a blow to the assumptions they based their security on. Their recovery may involve different issues and move at a different rate. They may be just going into crisis when the victim herself has begun to resolve the crisis, especially if there is a considerable time lag between the assault and its revelation to the family. They need warnings about their own safety, that they may experience severe sudden anger while driving that could cause them to do something dangerous. They also may have difficulty concentrating, reading, or working.

They need information about how long the recovery process may take, what danger signs such as alcohol use they can be aware of, and how to help the victim get the help she needs.

Take Care of Yourself

In our years of working in the rape crisis field we have seen the toll that the victimization of some takes on all of us, particularly those helping directly. Your own level of fear, anxiety and anger may be elevated. You can feel burdened and overwhelmed by the crisis and need. In some settings, such as a clinic or school counseling office, you may find yourself identified as *the one* to work with rape victims. You can quickly be overwhelmed by the victims coming forward. You also may find yourself processing an assault in your own past.

All of this can create a sense of urgency that leads you to forget your usual ways of taking care of yourself. You need self-care skills more than ever when you are working with victims. Don't let them go. Learn more. Find as many ways as you can to let go of the pain and anguish you take on from the victim. Sometimes making notes right away helps. Within the constraints of confidentiality, talking to another understanding person about your reactions might help.

Be aware that sometimes people helping victims protect themselves by seeing differences between themselves and the victims, creating "us/them" categories. This coping method interferes with working with victims. It is used to avoid examining your assumptions about the world that otherwise would be disturbed. Anyone can be victimized. Sexual violence may challenge your beliefs about people. If you examine your beliefs honestly, you will be better able to help those who are directly victimized.

It is courageous to look this problem in the face, see it as a danger to all of us, and help others be free of the shadows.

Appendix:

The First Few Hours

Please let it be a bad dream. Should I have a medical exam? What about pregnancy? Antibiotics? Can I just get the examination and not report? What if it has been days or weeks? Should I report it to the police or not.

PLEASE LET IT BE A BAD DREAM

You may be thinking, "Let it all be a nightmare, so it will all go away when I wake up again. Just let it be like it was before."

You may never have been as frightened of dying. You have survived a major threat to your life, for hours perhaps, or days.

It takes time for your system to react to a threat this big—even to begin to believe it.

"It couldn't have happened. Not now. Not to me. Not here. Not him."

What happened is real, and as you begin to grasp that, you face decisions about medical care, police reporting, and what to tell your family and friends.

FOR FAMILY AND FRIENDS

You will be in shock, too. Try not to add to her burden by losing control and trying to find and kill the rapist. She does not need to worry about you right now, and also will feel guilty for causing so much trouble.

SHOULD I HAVE A MEDICAL EXAM?

A medical examination serves several purposes for you. You may plan to report to the police, fear pregnancy, or want a prophylactic dose of antibiotics. It can reassure you that you are all right.

The medical examination is not an easy process. You may feel well taken care of by trained professionals, or you feel as if you are being raped again. Be sure to have a friend or advocate with you.

Take another set of clothes with you, or have someone meet you at the hospital with clothes. Yours may be taken for evidence.

You may wait for some time at the emergency room There will be forms to fill out and questions to answer.

Even if you have not yet decided about reporting to the police, the hospital staff will probably do the examination according to evidence gathering protocal. Evidence needs to be gathered as soon as possible. The medical staff will look for and document evidence of sexual contact, collecting samples of body fluids. Any signs of force or that a struggle occurred (bruises, torn clothing) would be noted. Some of this evidence will help identify the assailant: for example his blood type may be determined, or there may be particles or hairs he left behind. The doctor will look for any other injuries and provide treatment.

WHAT ABOUT PREGNANCY?

A test will be made to see if you are pregnant already. Later you will need to be tested again to see if you became pregnant as a result of the rape. Although some women have become pregnant as a result of rape, it is more likely that you will not.

You may be offered the "morning-after pill," a powerful dose of DES that keeps you from becoming pregnant in most cases. It is somewhat controversial. Sorting through the controversy is too difficult when you are in shock. If you know you don't want that treatment you can refuse it.

ANTIBIOTICS?

Contracting a sexually transmitted disease is a concern. This is also unlikely, but still a possibility. A test will be done to establish that you do not have syphillis or gonorrhea. There is treatment for each which may be provided immediately to prevent the development. You will be scheduled to be tested again at a later time. You will need to have those dates in writing and put them someplace easy to find. Your memory of this time will probably not be very good.

After the examination, have someone else drive you home. When people are in shock they are not able to pay full attention to anything.

Some hospital programs have trained counselors to aid rape victims and their families.

FOR FAMILY AND FRIENDS

If you are a sexual partner, you need to be concerned about sexually transmitted disease too.

This is a time to concentrate on concrete physical health care. This is an important process for her and her feelings about her body.

CAN I JUST GET THE EXAMINATION AND NOT REPORT?

You may want to check with your local rape crisis center about the requirements of the legal system. In some states hospitals are required to notify police when they treat victims of serious crimes. Under most circumstancs for *adults*, obtaining medical examination and reporting to the police are separate. If you get your medical examination at an emergency room of a hospital and the medical staff contacts the police, you are not required to talk to the police officer, or to sign the release of medical information form. Keep in mind that in most states Victim Compensation is only available when a police report is made.

If you go to a private doctor, or a clinic such as Planned Parenthood, the report to the police will be left entirely to you. If you are going some time after the assault your doctor doesn't even need to know that your symptoms are related—treatment for vaginitis is the same.

FOR FAMILY AND FRIENDS

Her concern may be her own privacy. *Who* knows *what* is up to her. Follow her lead. These decisions are hers.

WHAT IF IT HAS BEEN DAYS OR WEEKS?

Medical care is still a consideration even though several days or even weeks have passed since the rape.

You may have one of several medical problems. You may have experienced itching and vaginal discomfort. You may still be concerned about pregnancy. The dangers of sexually transmitted diseases, including AIDS, are obvious enough to create concern. Most rape victims are reassured by a medical examination done in circumstances that are respectful, and careful. It is usually too late to gather legal evidence after 2 days or so. Sometimes evidence of concern for physical well-being is considered during legal proceedings.

If you do decide to get medical care, take a friend or someone from a rape crisis center with you. Now is no time to expect yourself to be assertive with medical personnel. The decisions you are facing may be too difficult or embarassing to decide on your own. For example, do you want to take sleeping pills or ask for an alternative? How can the vaginal itching and irritation be taken care of? Is the sore throat a psychological reaction, or a physical problem? Why is your whole body still sore?

Turn a deaf ear to any remarks about rape victims. They do not apply to you. (Or any other rape victim.) You deserve some peace of mind from this examination, and some reassurances that you are okay.

SHOULD I REPORT IT TO THE POLICE OR NOT?

You may also be uncertain about reporting the rape to the police. Unfortunately you are making this tough decision in the midst of your crisis. If you want the chance to gather evidence of the rape, the first two days are the most important. If there is even a small chance you may later want to report to the police, it is useful to get a medical examination.

Do whatever makes you feel most powerful and in control and is most consistent with your need for community support and friendship. If you will feel stronger and more protected, report to the police. They are often much more sensitive than they are portrayed to be in books and on television. They will do their best to do their jobs, which is to collect evidence and identify the person who committed the crime. They may be able to arrest him, and may not.

Although others may make you feel so, it is not your responsibility to stop a rapist. You did not create him; he is not your responsibility. If you report to the police, he may be stopped, but he may not be. Even the police are frustrated with how helpless they sometimes are to move against known offenders.

FOR FAMILY AND FRIENDS

Ask her if you can call a rape crisis center for information and support.

Resources

Suggested Readings

Each of these books is helpful for understanding rape and sexual violence without being clinically oriented or overloaded with case histories.

BOOKS ABOUT RECOVER FROM SEXUAL ASSAULT

Benedict, Helen. *Recovery: How to Survive Sexual Assault for Women, Men, Teenagers, and Their Friends and Families.* New York: Doubleday and Company, 1985.

Johnson, Kathryn M. *If You Are Raped: What Every Woman Needs To Know.* Holmes Beach, FL: Learning Publications, Inc., 1985.

Katz, Judy H. *No Fairy Godmothers, No Magic Wands: The Healing Process After Rape.* Saratoga, CA: R & E Publishers, 1984.

Ledray, Linda E. *Recovering From Rape.* New York: Henry Holt and Company, 1986.

McEvoy, Alan W., and Brookings, Jeff B. *If She Is Raped: A Book For Husbands, Fathers, and Male Friends.* Holmes Beach, FL: Learning Publications, Inc., 1985.

NiCarthy, Ginny. *Getting Free: A Handbook for Women in Abusive Relationships.* Seattle, WA: Seal Press, 1982

BOOKS ABOUT RECOVERY FROM CHILD SEXUAL ABUSE

Adams, Caren and Fay, Jennifer. *Recovering From Child Sexual Abuse: A Guide for Parents and Children* (title tentative). Seattle, WA: University of Washington Press, 1990.

Bass, Ellen and Davis, Laura. *Courage To Heal: A Guide For Women Survivors of Child Sexual Abuse*. New York: Harper and Row, 1988.

Byerly, Carolyn M. *The Mother's Book: How to Survive the Incest of Your Child*. Dubuque, IA: Kendall/Hunt, 1985

Daugherty, Lynn B. *Why Me? Help for Victims of Child Sexual Abuse (Even If They Are Adults Now)*. Racine, WI: Mother Courage Press, 1984.

Gil, Eliana. *Outgrowing the Pain: A Book for and about Adults Abused as Children*. San Francisco, CA: Launch Press, 1983.

Lew, Mike. *Victims No Longer: Men Recovering From Incest*. New York: Nevraumont Press, 1988.

Maltz, Wendy and Holman, Beverly. *Incest and Sexuality: A Guide To Understanding and Healing*. Lexington, MA: Lexington Books, 1987.

Woititz, Janet G. *Healing Your Sexual Self*. Deerfield Beach, FL: Health Communications, Inc., 1989.

BOOKS ABOUT RAPE

Adams, Caren; Fay, Jennifer; and Loreen-Martin, Jan. *No Is Not Enough: Helping Teenagers Avoid Sexual Assault*. San Luis Obispo, CA: Impact Publishers, 1984.

Butler, Sandra. *Conspiracy of Silence: The Trauma of Incest.* Volcano, CA: Volcano Press, 1985.

Estrich, Susan. *Real Rape: How the Legal System Victimizes Women Who Say No.* Cambridge, MA: Harvard University Press, 1987.

Finkelhor, David and Yllo, Kersti. *License to Rape: Sexual Abuse of Wives.* New York: The Free Press, 1985.

Fortune, Marie. *Sexual Violence: The Unmentionable Sin, An Ethical and Pastoral Perspective.* New York: The Pilgrim Press, 1983.

Griffin, Susan. *Rape: The Power of Consciousness.* San Francisco, CA: Harper and Row, 1979.

Lederer, Laura (Editor). *Take Back the Night: Women On Pornography.* New York: William Morrow, 1980.

Malamuth, Neil M. and Donnerstein, Edward. *Pornography and Sexual Aggression.* Orlando, FL: Academic Press, 1984.

Medea, Andra and Thompson, Kathleen. *Against Rape.* New York: Farrar, Straus, and Giroux, 1974.

Pellaver, Mary D.; Chester, Barbara; and Boyajian, Jane (Editors). *Sexual Assault and Abuse: A Handbook for Clergy and Religious Professionals.* San Francisco, CA: Harper and Row, 1987.

Russell, Diana E. H. *Rape In Marriage.* New York: Macmillan, 1982.

Russell, Diana E. H. *The Politics Of Rape: The Victim's Perspective.* New York: Stein and Day, 1975.

White, Evelyn C. *Chain Chain Change: For Black Women Dealing With Physical and Emotional Abuse.* Seattle, WA: The Seal Press, 1985.

Zambrano, Myrna M. *Mejor Sola Que Mal Acompanada: Para la Mujer Golpeada/For the Latina in an Abusive Relationship.* Seattle, WA: The Seal Press, 1985.

BOOKS ABOUT OFFENDERS

Beneke, Timothy. Men *On Rape: What They Have To Say About Sexual Violence.* New York: St. Martin's, 1982.

Carnes, Patrick. *Out of Shadows: Understand Sexual Addiction.* Minneapolis, MN: Compcare Publications, 1983.

Support Groups

There are support groups in most areas for rape survivors and for their friends and families. To locate one, call your local Rape Crisis Center. If you are not aware of a local Center, look in the phone book under Rape or Crisis/Hotlines.

The office of the National Coalition Against Sexual Assault, in Washington, D.C. is also able to tell you whether or not there is a center in your area.

Write or call:

National Coalition Against Sexual Assault (NCASA)
2428 Ontario Rd., N.W.
Washington, DC 20009
(202) 483-7165

Or, try the phone book under Women's Services, Men's Services, Youth Services, Children's Services, Counseling/Mental Health, Crisis Hotlines, Women's Shelters,Battered Women,YWCA. Support and Self-Help Groups, Victim's Assistance, or Crime Prevention. Calling a few of these agencies will probably locate someone who knows what support groups are available in your area.

There are some counties that have Victim's Assistance Units within the Prosecutor's Office. If there is one in your area, the staff may be aware of what groups are available. Call your county courthouse. Or contact:

National Organization for Victim Assistance (NOVA)
717 D Street, N.W.
Washington, DC 20004
(202) 393-6682
They have a listing of the Victim's Assistance Units within local Prosecutor's Offices.

Family and Friends of Missing Persons and Violent Crime Victims
P.O. Box 27529
Seattle, WA 98125
(206) 362-1081
in Washington 1-800-346-7555
They have the same listing that NOVA uses, and can check for an office in your state and area.

Writing or calling the following organizations may also help you to locate a support group in your area.

Incest Resources
Women's Center
46 Pleasant St.
Cambridge, MA 12139
(617) 492-1818.
Call this number to schedule a training only, other-wise please write a letter.

VOICES (Victims of Incest Can Emerge Survivors) in Action, Inc.
P.O. Box 148309
Chicago. IL 60614
(312) 327-1500
Primarily a source for groups in your area for incest survivors, but can also help locate someone in your area who knows what other groups are available.

Looking Up
P.O. Box K
Augusta, ME 04330
(207) 626-3402
Primarily able to help in the New England area, but may also in other states.

Other New Harbinger Self-Help Titles

The Relaxation & Stress Reduction Workbook, $12.95
Leader's Guide to the Relaxation & Stress Reduction Workbook,
    $14.95
Thoughts & Feelings: The Art of Cognitive Stress Intervention, $11.95
Messages: The Communication Skills Book, $11.95
The Divorce Book, $10.95
Hypnosis for Change: A Manual of Proven Techniques, $11.95
The Deadly Diet: Recovering from Anorexia & Bulimia, $10.95
Self-Esteem, $11.95
Beyond Grief, $11.95
Chronic Pain Control Workbook, 12.95
Rekindling Desire, $10.95
Life Without Fear: Anxiety and Its Cure, $9.95
Visualization for Change, $11.95
Guideposts to Meaning, $10.95
Controlling Stagefright, $10.95
Videotape: Hypnosis for Relaxation, $24.95
Starting Out Right: Essential Parenting Skills for Your Child's First Seven
    Years, $12.95
Big Kids: A Parent's Guide to Weight Control for Children, $10.95
Personal Peace: Transcending Your Interpersonal Limits, $10.95
My Parent's Keeper: Adult Children of the Emotionally Disturbed, $10.95
When Anger Hurts, $11.95
Free of the Shadows: Recovering from Sexual Violence, $10.95
Resolving Conflict With Others and Within Yourself, $11.95
Lifetime Weight Control, $10.95

Send a check or purchase order for the titles you want,
plus $1.50 for shipping and handling, to:

New Harbinger Publications
Department B
5674 Shattuck Avenue
Oakland, CA 94609

**Or write for our free catalog of all our quality self-help
publications.**